A-Z CRAW

CW00670453

CONTENTS

Key to Map Pages	2-3
Map Pages	4-37

Index
Villages, Stations, Hospitals
& selected Places of Interest

REFERENCE

Motorway	**M23**	Airport	✈
A Road	**A2220**	Car Park (selected)	P
B Road	**B2036**	Church or Chapel	†
Dual Carriageway		Cycle Route (selected)	ᗧᗧ
One-way Street Traffic flow on A Roads is also indicated by a heavy line on the driver's left.	→	Fire Station	■
		Hospital	⊕
		House Numbers (A & B Roads only)	55 64
Road Under Construction Opening dates are correct at the time of publication		Information Centre	ℹ
Proposed Road		National Grid Reference	⁵30
Restricted Access		Park & Ride	Hop Oast P+R
Pedestrianized Road		Police Station	▲
Track / Footpath	- - - - -	Post Office	★
Residential Walkway	•••••••	Safety Camera with Speed Limit Fixed cameras and long term road works cameras. Symbols do not indicate camera direction.	㉚

Railway	Station ⚏ Tunnel ⚎ Level Crossing	Toilet:
		  without facilities for the Disabled
		  with facilities for the Disabled
			▽
			▽

Built-up Area	CHURCH ST.	Educational Establishment	▨
Local Authority Boundary	— · — · —	Hospital or Healthcare Building	▨
Posttown Boundary	————	Industrial Building	▢
Postcode Boundary (within Posttown)	— — — —	Leisure or Recreational Facility	▨
		Place of Interest	▨
		Public Building	▨
Map Continuation	▲ 16	Shopping Centre or Market	▨
		Other Selected Buildings	▢

SCALE

1:15,840
4 inches to 1 mile

0	¼	½ Mile

6.31 cm to 1 km
10.16 cm to 1 mile

0	250	500	750	1 Kilometre

Copyright of Geographers' A-Z Map Company Limited

Fairfield Road, Borough Green, Sevenoaks, Kent TN15 8PP
Telephone: 01732 781000 (Enquiries & Trade Sales)
                  01732 783422 (Retail Sales)

www.az.co.uk
Copyright © Geographers' A-Z Map Co. Ltd.
Edition 6 2012

OS Ordnance Survey® This product includes mapping data licensed from Ordnance Survey® with the permission of the Controller of Her Majesty's Stationery Office.

© Crown Copyright 2011. All rights reserved. Licence number 100017302
Safety camera information supplied by www.PocketGPSWorld.com
Speed Camera Location Database Copyright 2011 © PocketGPSWorld.com

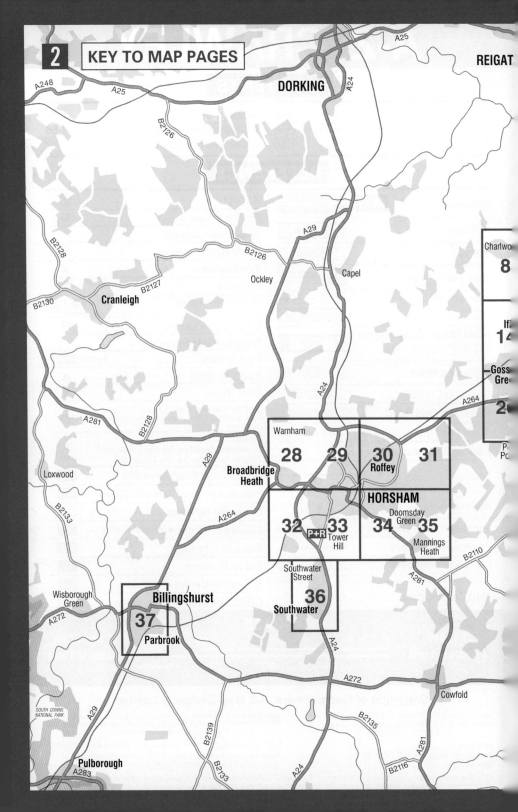

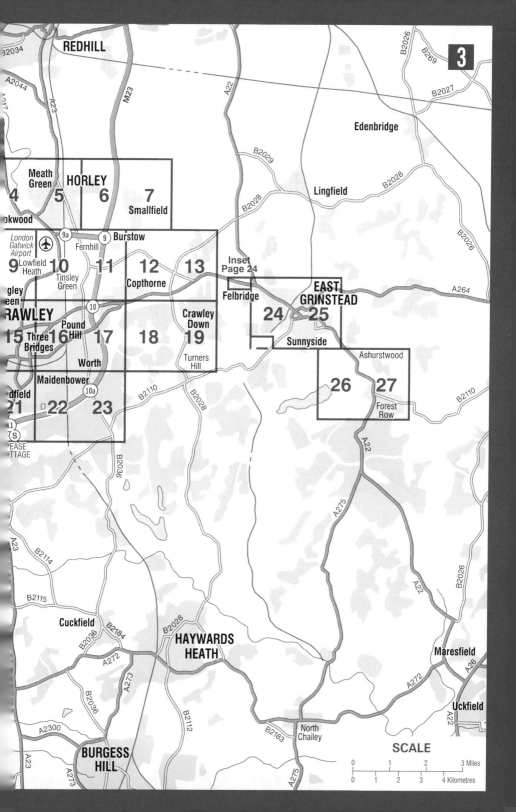

REDHILL

3

B2034

A2044

A2026

B269

B2027

Edenbridge

Meath
Green

HORLEY

4 **5** **6** **7**
Smallfield

okwood

B2029

B2028

Lingfield

B2028

B2026

*London
Gatwick
Airport*
Lowfield
Heath

Burstow

9a 9 Fernhill

9 **10** **11** **12** **13**

Tinsley
Green

Copthorne

**Inset
Page 24**

Felbridge

**EAST
GRINSTEAD**

A264

gley
een

RAWLEY

10

Pound
Hill

Crawley
Down

24 **25**

15 **16** **17** **18** **19**

Three
Bridges

Worth

Turners
Hill

Sunnyside

Ashurstwood

dfield

Maidenbower

10a

21 **22** **23**

B2110

B2028

26 **27**

Forest
Row

B2110

EASE
TTAGE

A22

B2036

A275

A23

B2114

A22

B2026

B2115

Cuckfield

B2184

B2028

**HAYWARDS
HEATH**

Maresfield

A26

B2036

A272

A273

A272

B2036

Uckfield

A22

B2112

North
Chailey

SCALE

A2300

B2183

0   1   2   3 Miles

**BURGESS
HILL**

A273

A2300

A275

0 1 2 3   4 Kilometres

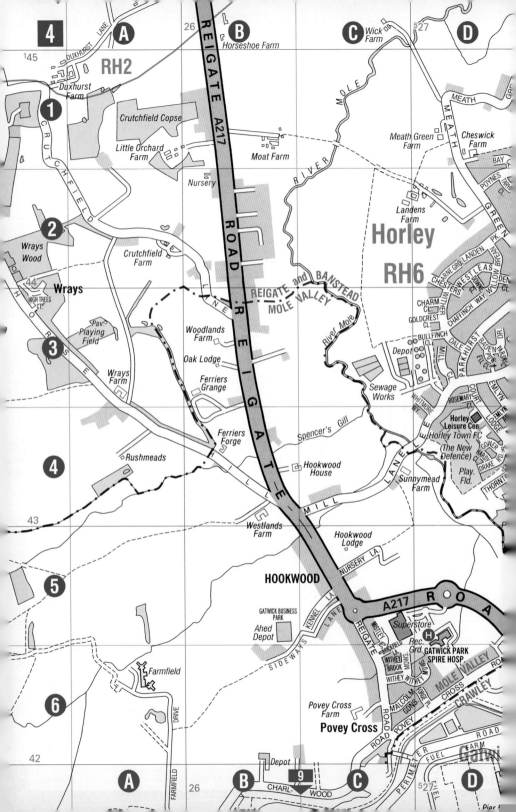

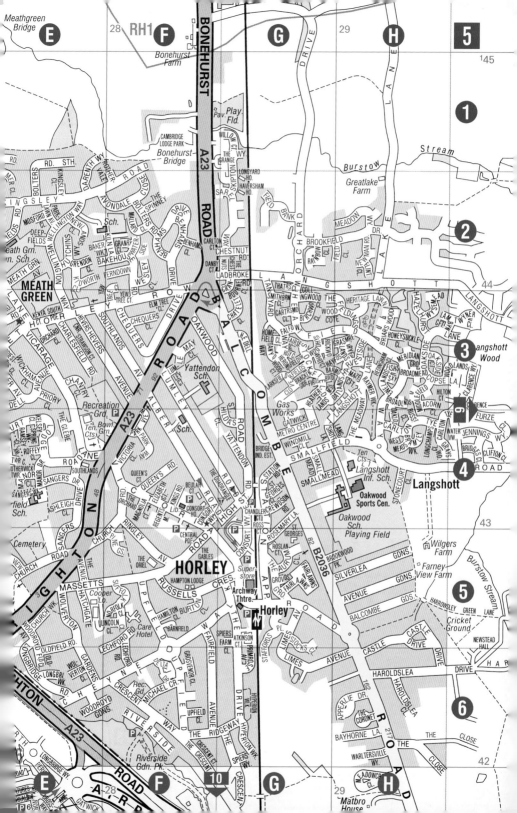

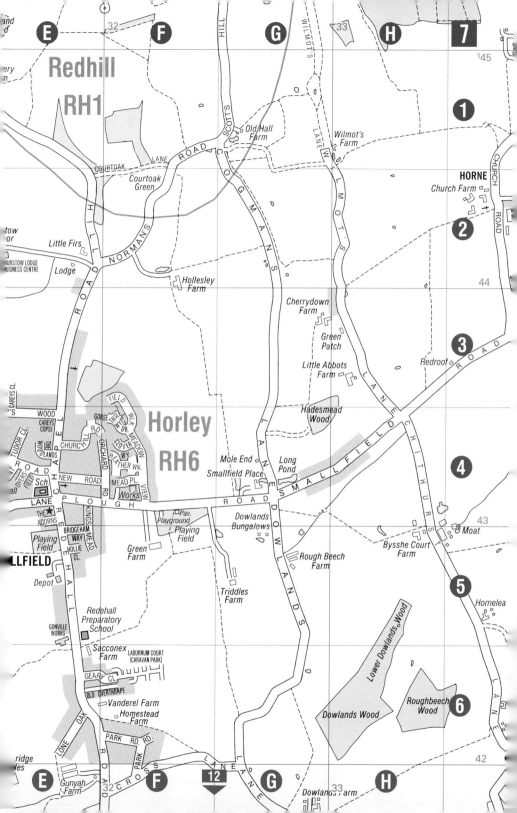

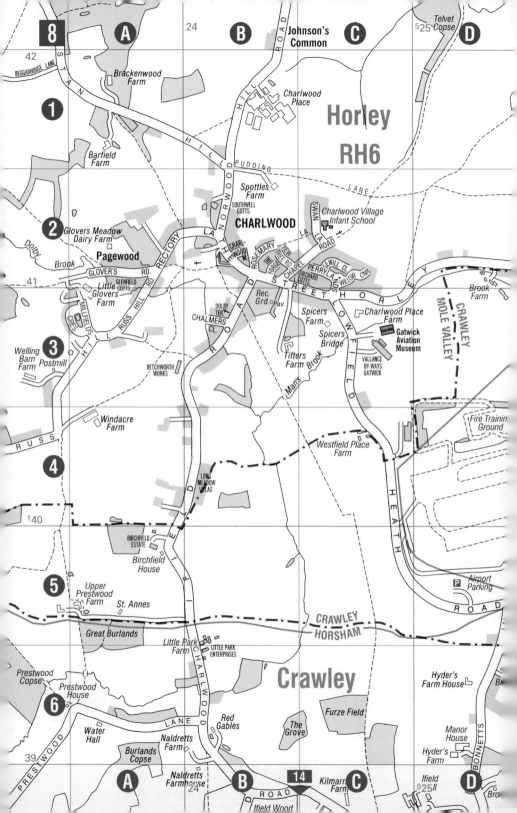

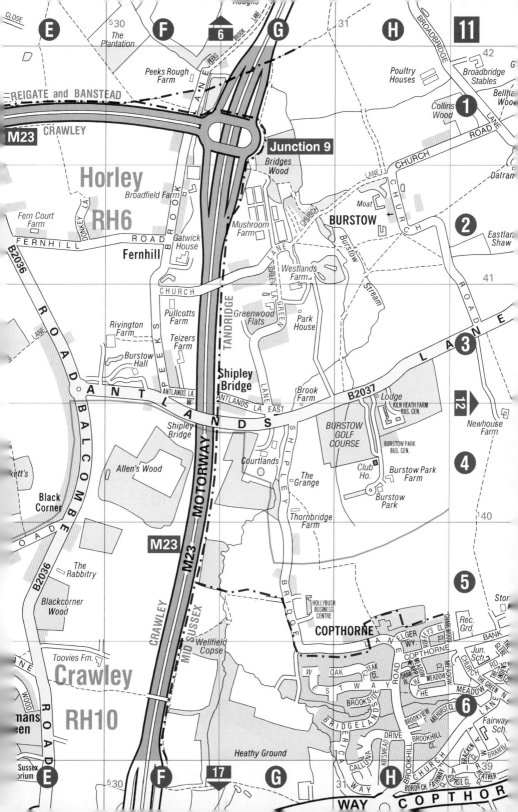

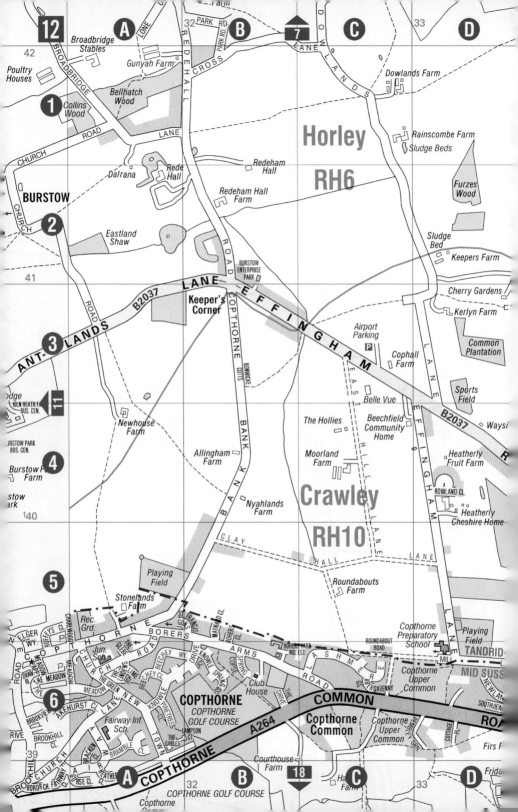

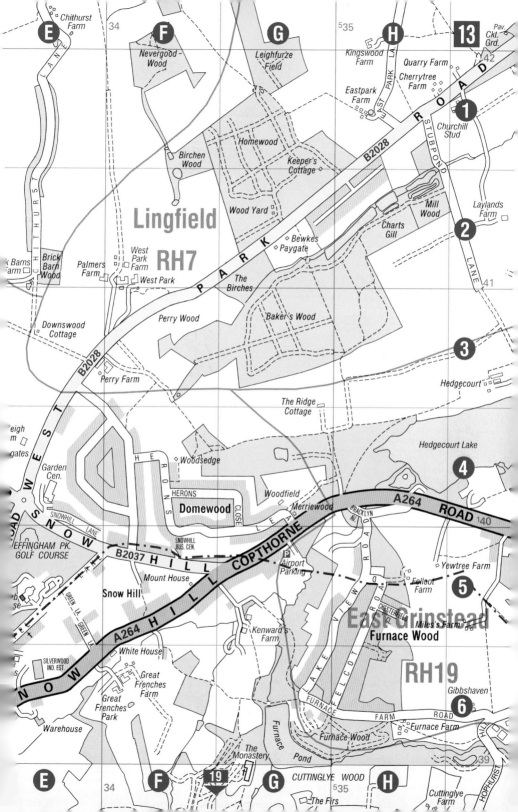

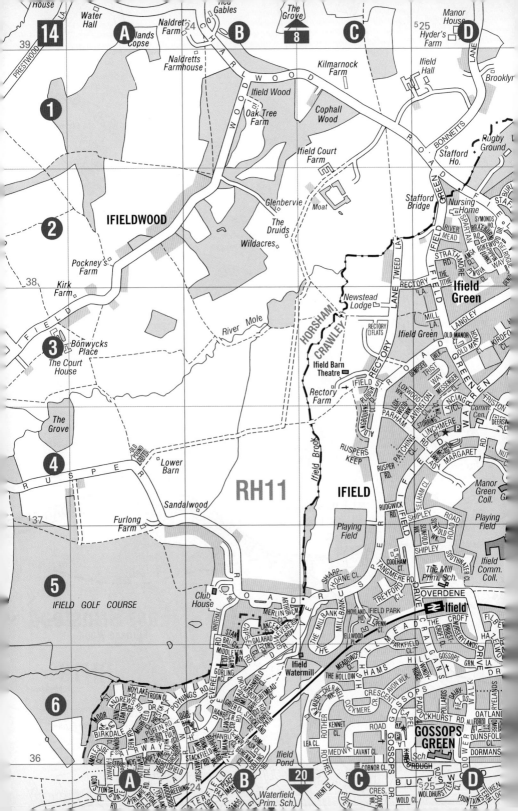

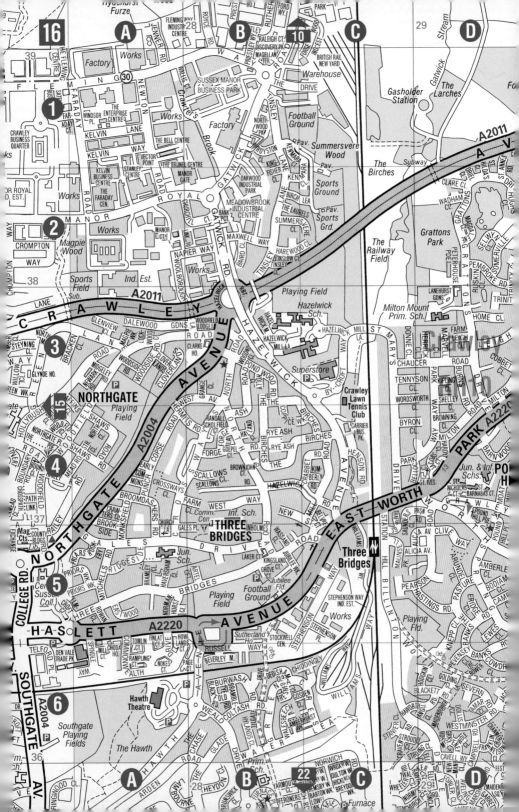

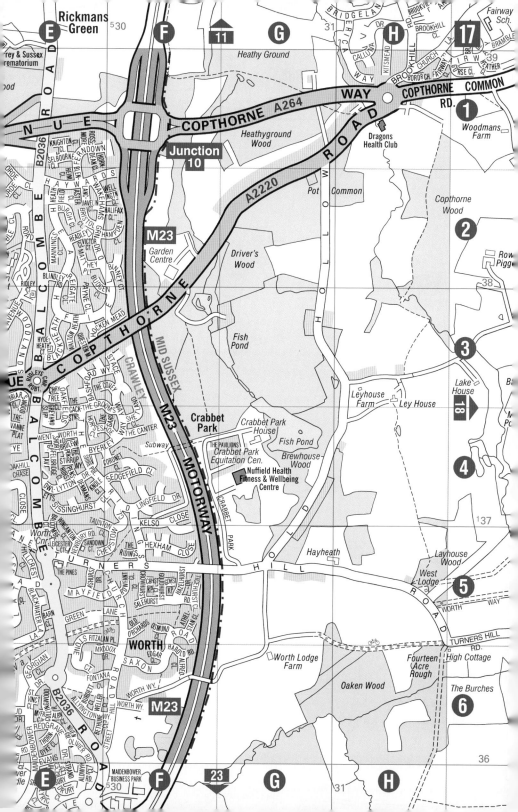

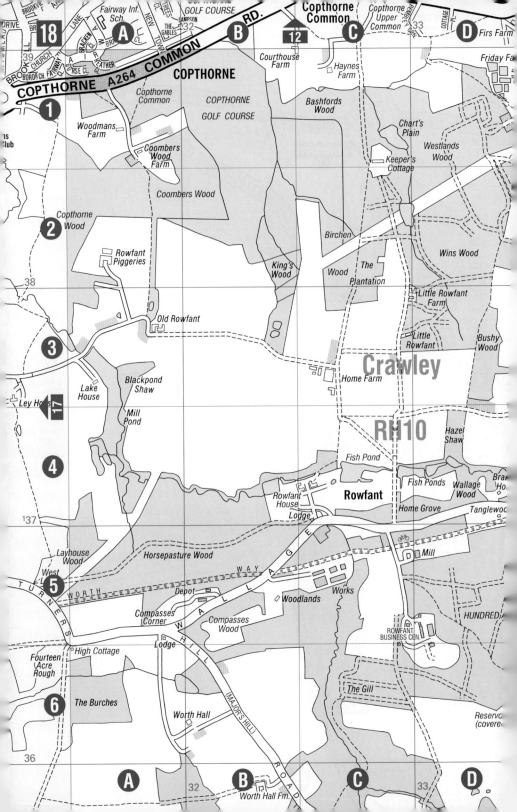

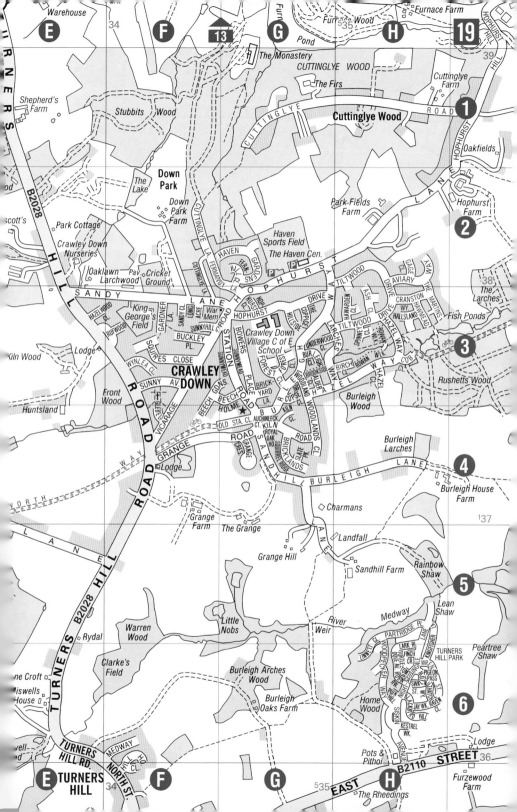

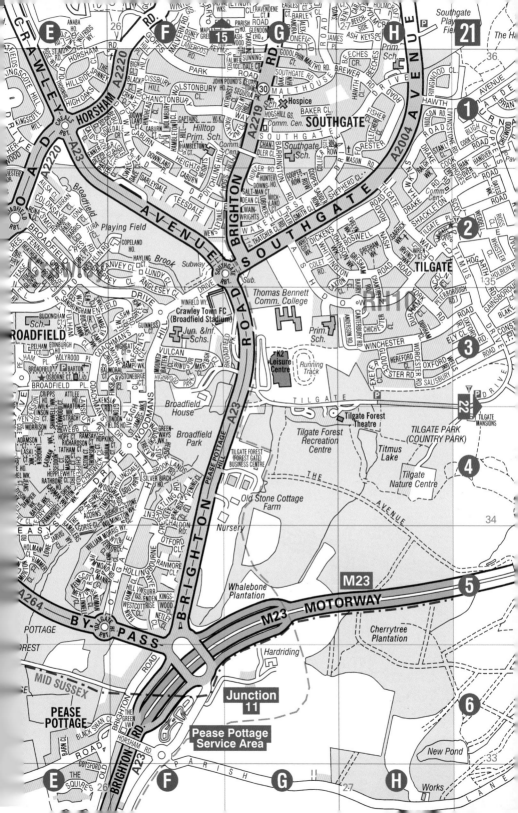

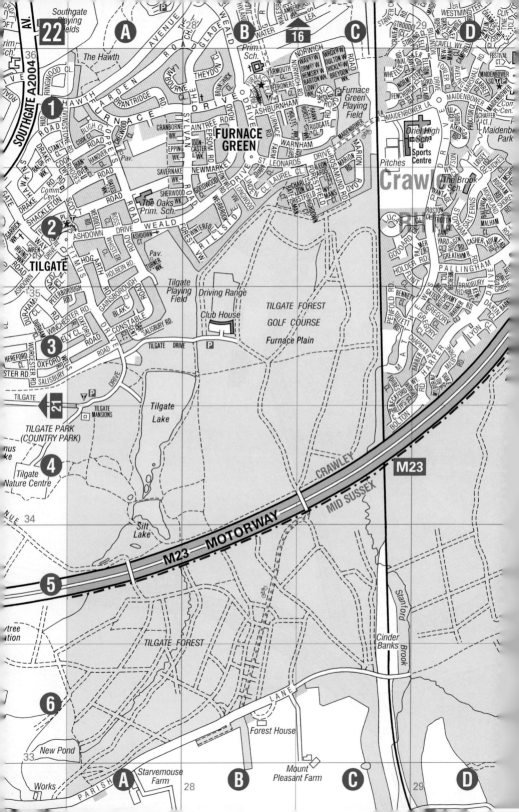

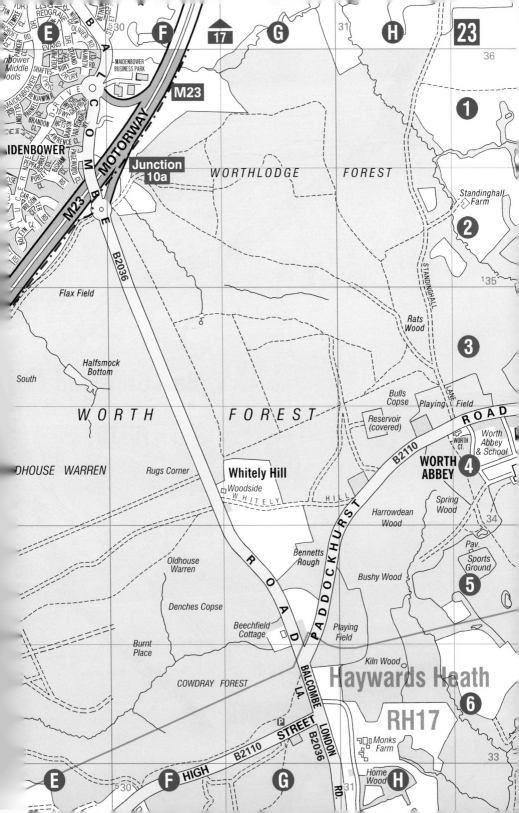

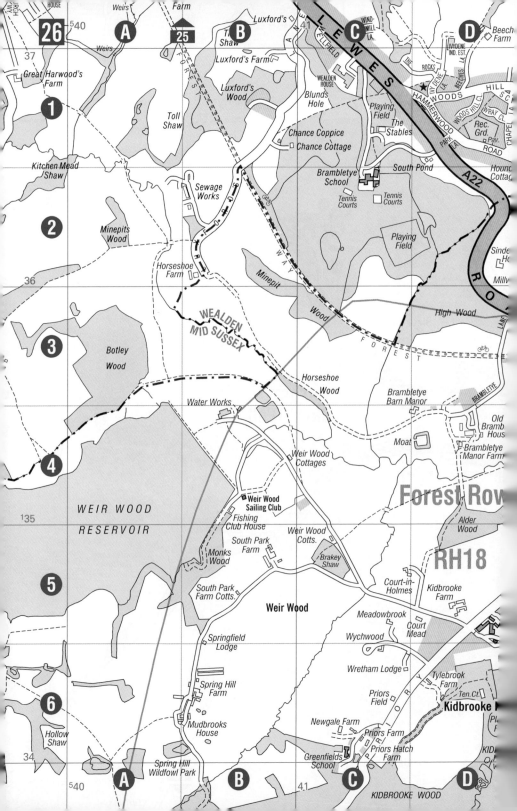

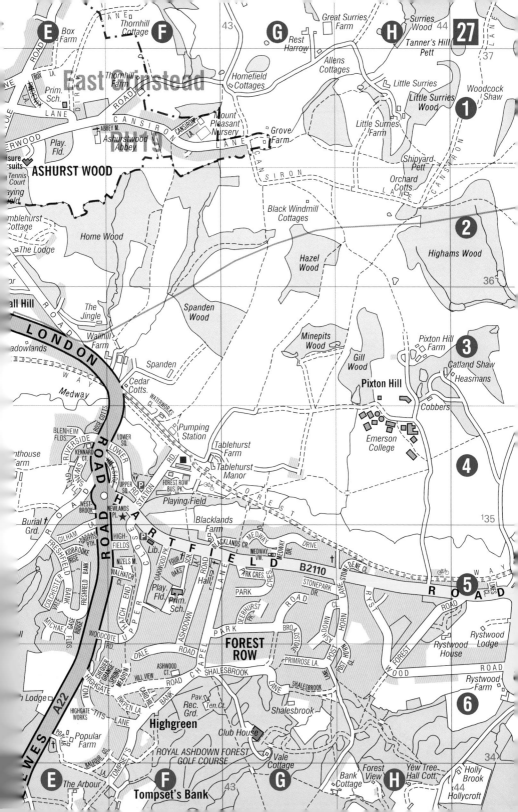

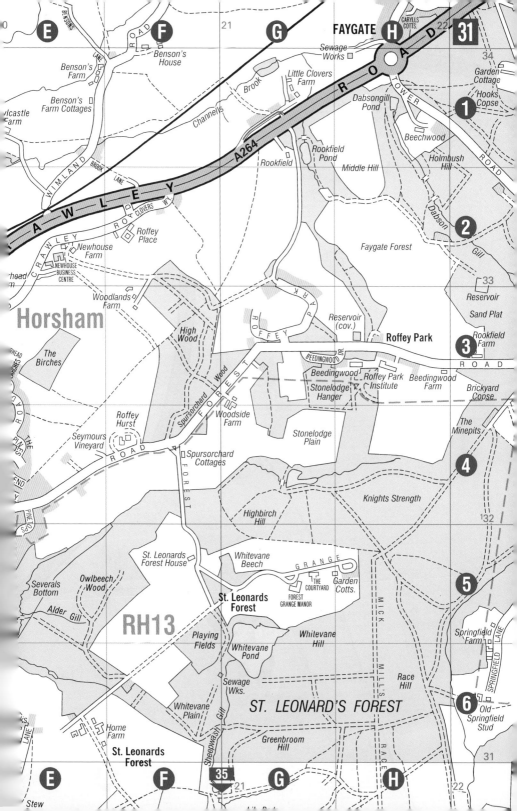

Map of Horsham / St. Leonard's Forest area

E **F** **G** **FAYGATE** **H** **ROAD** **31**

21 | CARYLLS COTTS. | 22 | 34

BENSONS LANE

Benson's House

Benson's Farm

Sewage Works

Little Clovers Farm

Garden Cottage

Hooks Copse

1

Benson's Farm Cottages

Brook

Channels

Dabsongill Pond

Beechwood

lcastle Farm

WIMLAND BROOK

ROY LANE

A264 CRAWLEY

Rookfield

Rookfield Pond

Middle Hill

Holmbush Hill

TOWER ROAD

Dabson Gill

2

CLOVERS WY.

Roffey Place

Faygate Forest

33

Reservoir

Sand Plat

CRAWLEY

Newhouse Farm

NEWHOUSE BUSINESS CENTRE

head m

Woodlands Farm

ROFFEY PARK

Reservoir (cov.)

Roffey Park

Rookfield Farm

3

Horsham

The Birches

High Wood

Spursorchard Wood

FOREST

BEEDINGWOOD DR.

Beedingwood

Roffey Park Institute

Stonelodge Hanger

Beedingwood Farm

R O A D

Brickyard Copse

THE ROAD

PINGS

Roffey Hurst

Seymours Vineyard

Woodside Farm

Stonelodge Plain

The Minepits

4

PINE S.

ROAD

Spursorchard Cottages

FOREST

Highbirch Hill

Knights Strength

132

St. Leonards Forest House

Whitevane Beech

GRANGE

THE COURTYARD

Garden Cotts.

5

Severals Bottom

Owlbeech Wood

St. Leonards Forest

FOREST GRANGE MANOR

MICK

Springfield Farm

SPRINGFIELD LANE

Alder Gill

RH13

Playing Fields

Whitevane Pond

Whitevane Hill

MILL'S DRIVE

Race Hill

Old Springfield Stud

6

Whitevane Plain

Sewage Wks.

ST. LEONARD'S FOREST

RACE

LANE

Home Farm

Greenbroom Hill

31

St. Leonards Forest

SHEEPWASH GILL

E **F** **35** **G** **H**

21 | 22

Stew

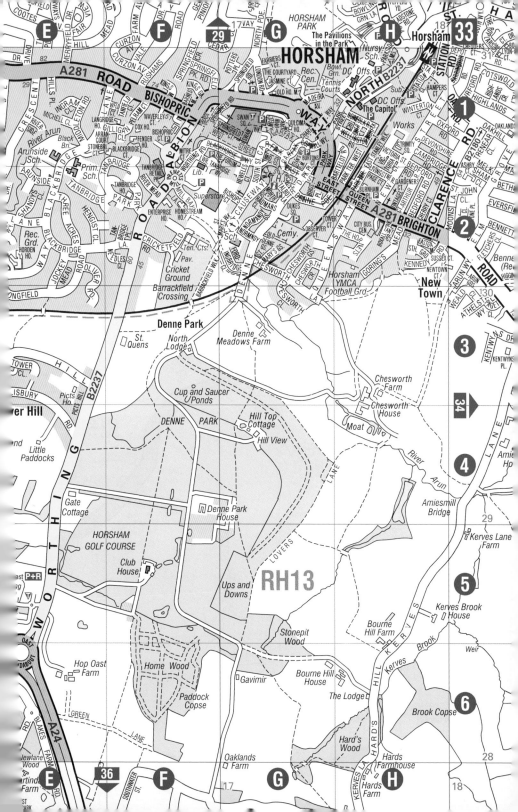

HORSHAM

34

St. Leonards Park

Horsham

RH13

Coolhurst

Oakhill

New Town

Grid references: A B C D along top and bottom; 1 2 3 4 5 6 down the left side.

Roads and labels include:
HARWOOD, STA. RD., OAKHILL RD., CLARENCE RD., BRIGHTON ROAD (B2180), ELM, B2180, COTSWOLD CT. CL., POTTER'S, HIGHLANDS AV., GROVE, MACLEOD RD., BETHUNE, EVERSFIELD, ORCHARD RD., HORNBEAM CL., LAUREL WK., BENNETTS, HIGGINS WAY, ST. LEONARD'S, DICKINS WAY, HERNBROOK DR., SANDEMAN, KENTWYNS DR., KENTWYNS PL., OAKLAND CL., HORN BROOK, HORNBROOK HILL, HORNBROOK COPSE, COMPTONS ROAD, GHYLL CR., HAMMERPOND ROAD, HERON ROAD, HERON WAY, GREBE CRESCENT, BRAMBLING RD., DOOMSDAY WAY, DOOMSDAY GDN., DOOMSDAY LANE, ACREMAN WAY, COOL. HURST LA., MANOR, COPPERFIELDS, A281, SEDGWICK LANE, BUCKLEY, KERVES LANE, KERVES BROOK

Places of interest:
Millais Sch., Sports Cen., Play. Fld., Forest Recreational Centre, The Forest Sch., Smiths Barn Farm Play. Fld., Heron Way Prim. Sch., Reservoir (covered), Sandpit Clump, Golden Folly, Townhouse Copse, Highland Copse, The Glen, Playing Field, Rugby Ground, Doomsday Bridge, Doomsday Green, Hornbrook Farm, Coolhurst Grange, Copperfields Manor, Huxley's (Bird of Prey & Garden), Hornbrook Nurseries, Garden House, Amiesmill House, White's Bridge, Amiesmill Farm, Whitesbridge Farm, Kerves Lane Farm, Kerves Brook House, Oakdean Nursery, Corner Wood, Birchen Bri., Pavilion Wood, Sheep Wood, Birchenbridge House, Rickfield Farm, Ashwins, Whytings Farm, Landlord's Copse, Bulls Farm, Brook Copse, Weir, High Wood, Bushy Copse, Furze Field, Kites Copse, Amiesmill Bridge, River Arun, Kerves Brook

Motorway/road markers: 31, 30, 33, 32, 130, 29, 28, 18, 19

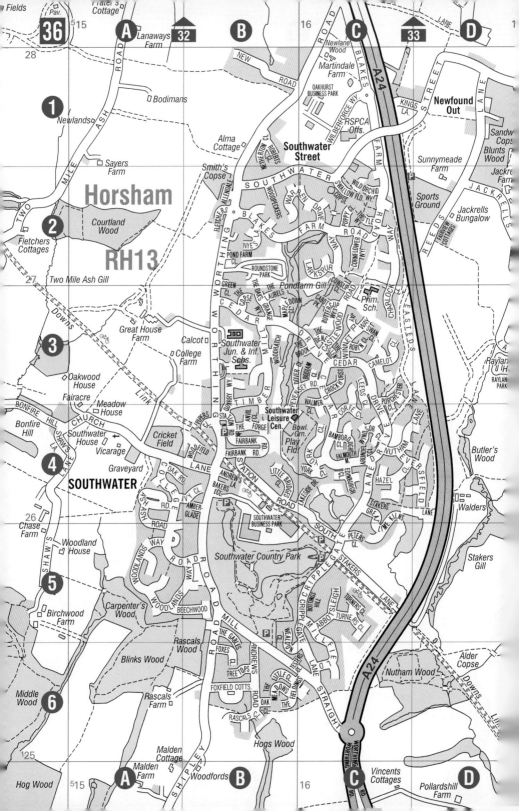

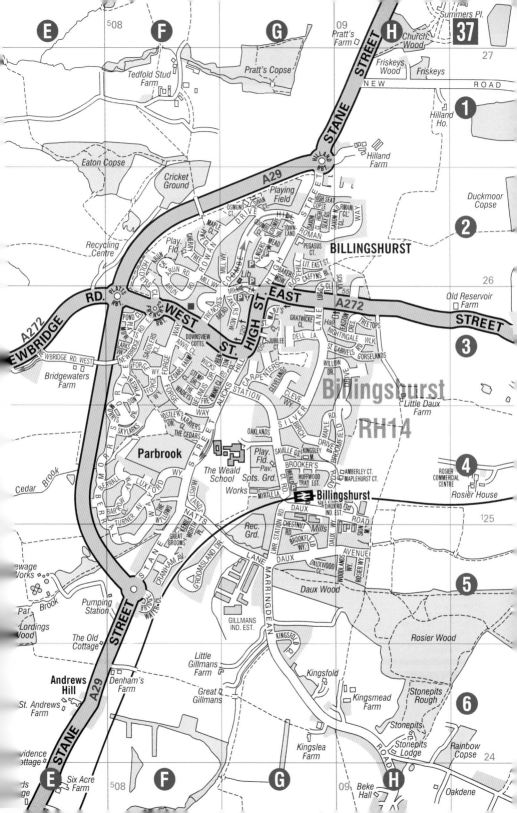

INDEX

Including Streets, Places & Areas, Hospitals etc., Industrial Estates,
Selected Flats & Walkways, Service Areas, Stations and Selected Places of Interest.

HOW TO USE THIS INDEX

1. Each street name is followed by its Postcode District and then by its Locality abbreviation(s) and then by its map reference;
e.g. **Albany Rd.** RH11: Craw . . . .5E **15** is in the RH11 Postcode District and the Crawley Locality and is to be found in square 5E on page **15**.
The page number is shown in bold type.

2. A strict alphabetical order is followed in which Av., Rd., St., etc. (though abbreviated) are read in full and as part of the street name;
e.g. **Barn Field Pl.** appears after **Barnfield** but before **Barnfield Rd.**

3. Streets and a selection of flats and walkways that cannot be shown on the mapping, appear in the index with the thoroughfare to which they are
connected shown in brackets; e.g. **Adversane Ct.** RH12: Hors . . . .5H **29** (off Blenheim Rd.)

4. Addresses that are in more than one part are referred to as not continuous.

5. Places and areas are shown in the index in **BLUE TYPE** and the map reference is to the actual map square in which the town centre or area is
located and not to the place name shown on the map; e.g. **ASHURST WOOD** 1D **26**

6. An example of a selected place of interest is **Crawley Museum Cen.** 6F **15**

7. An example of a station is **Billingshurst Station (Rail)** . . . .4G **37**, also included is **Park & Ride**.
e.g. **Hop Oast (Horsham) (Park & Ride)** 5E **33**

8. Service Areas are shown in the index in **BOLD CAPITAL TYPE**; e.g. **PEASE POTTAGE SERVICE AREA** 6F **21**

9. An example of a Hospital, Hospice or selected Healthcare facility is **CRAWLEY HOSPITAL** 5F **15**

GENERAL ABBREVIATIONS

All. : Alley	**Gdns.** : Gardens	**Pk.** : Park
App. : Approach	**Ga.** : Gate	**Pas.** : Passage
Av. : Avenue	**Gt.** : Great	**Pl.** : Place
Bri. : Bridge	**Grn.** : Green	**Pct.** : Precinct
Bldgs. : Buildings	**Gro.** : Grove	**Ri.** : Rise
Bungs. : Bungalows	**Hgts.** : Heights	**Rd.** : Road
Bus. : Business	**Ho.** : House	**Rdbt.** : Roundabout
Cen. : Centre	**Ind.** : Industrial	**Shop.** : Shopping
Cl. : Close	**Info.** : Information	**Sth.** : South
Comn. : Common	**Intl.** : International	**Sq.** : Square
Cnr. : Corner	**La.** : Lane	**St.** : Street
Cotts. : Cottages	**Lit.** : Little	**Ter.** : Terrace
Ct. : Court	**Lwr.** : Lower	**Twr.** : Tower
Cres. : Crescent	**Mnr.** : Manor	**Trad.** : Trading
Cft. : Croft	**Mans.** : Mansions	**Va.** : Vale
Dr. : Drive	**Mdw.** : Meadow	**Vw.** : View
E. : East	**Mdws.** : Meadows	**Vs.** : Villas
Ent. : Enterprise	**M.** : Mews	**Wlk.** : Walk
Est. : Estate	**Mt.** : Mount	**W.** : West
Fld. : Field	**Mus.** : Museum	**Yd.** : Yard
Flds. : Fields	**Nth.** : North	
Gdn. : Garden	**Pde.** : Parade	

LOCALITY ABBREVIATIONS

Adv : **Adversane**	F Row : **Forest Row**	Out : **Outwood**
Ash W : **Ashurst Wood**	Gatw : **Gatwick**	Pease P : **Pease Pottage**
Bal : **Balcombe**	Hookw : **Hookwood**	Plum P : **Plummers Plain**
Bill : **Billingshurst**	Horl : **Horley**	Rowf : **Rowfant**
Broad H : **Broadbridge Heath**	Horne : **Horne**	Salf : **Salfords**
Bur : **Burstow**	Hors : **Horsham**	Ship B : **Shipley Bridge**
Charlw : **Charlwood**	Ifield : **Ifield**	Sid : **Sidlow**
Colg : **Colgate**	Itch : **Itchingfield**	Slinf : **Slinfold**
Copt : **Copthorne**	Lwr Bee : **Lower Beeding**	Smallf : **Smallfield**
Craw : **Crawley**	Low H : **Lowfield Heath**	Southw : **Southwater**
Craw D : **Crawley Down**	Mann H : **Mannings Heath**	Turn H : **Turners Hill**
E Grin : **East Grinstead**	Monks G : **Monks Gate**	Warnh : **Warnham**
Fay : **Faygate**	Newchap : **Newchapel**	Worth : **Worth**
Felb : **Felbridge**	Nor H : **Norwood Hill**	

A

Abbey M. RH19: Ash W 1F **27**
Abbotsbury Ct. RH13: Hors 6A **30**
Abbotsfield Rd. RH11: Ifield 6A **14**
Abbotsleigh RH13: Southw 5C **36**
Abergavenny Gdns.
  RH10: Copt 6C **12**
Abinger Keep RH6: Horl 3H **5**
           (off Langshott La.)
Abrahams Rd. RH11: Craw 4D **20**

Acorn Cl. RH6: Horl 3H **5**
  RH19: E Grin 5E **25**
Acorns RH13: Hors 5C **30**
Acorns, The
  RH6: Smallf 4E **7**
  RH11: Craw 4E **21**
Adamson Ct. RH11: Craw 4E **21**
Adelaide Cl. RH11: Craw 2G **15**
  RH12: Hors 5B **30**
Adelphi Cl. RH10: Craw 1E **23**
Admiral Rd. RH11: Craw 2D **20**
Adrian Ct. RH11: Craw 4E **21**

Adversane Ct. RH12: Hors 5H **2**
           (off Blenheim R
Agate La. RH12: Hors 4A **2**
Ailsa Cl. RH11: Craw 2E **2**
Aintree Rd. RH10: Craw 1B **2**
Airport Way RH6: Gatw 1B
Akehurst Cl. RH10: Copt 6H
Albany Rd. RH11: Craw 5E
Alberta Dr. RH6: Smallf 4D
Albert Crane Ct. RH11: Craw 3D
Albert Rd. RH6: Horl 3
Albery Cl. RH12: Hors 5F

Albion Cl. RH10: Craw 6E 17
Albion Way RH12: Hors 1F 33
Albury Keep *RH6: Horl* *4G 5*
     (off Langshott La.)
Alder Cl. RH10: Craw D 3G 19
Alder Copse RH12: Hors 3D 32
Alders Av. RH19: E Grin 2D 24
Alders Vw. Dr. RH19: E Grin 2E 25
Aldingbourne Cl. RH11: Ifield 4C 14
Aldwych Cl. RH10: Craw 1E 23
Alexandra Ct. RH10: Craw 6G 15
Alfred Cl. RH10: Worth 6F 17
Alice Crocker Ho. RH19: E Grin 3E 25
Alicia Av. RH10: Craw 5C 16
Alicks Hill RH14: Bill 3G 37
Allcard Cl. RH12: Hors 5H 29
Allcot Cl. RH11: Craw 2B 20
Allendale RH13: Southw 2B 36
Allen's Cl. RH19: Ash W 1D 26
Allford Ct. RH11: Craw 6D 14
Allingham Gdns. RH12: Hors 4D 30
Allyington Way RH10: Worth 6E 17
Almond Cl. RH11: Craw 6D 14
Alpha Rd. RH11: Craw 5F 15
Alpine Walks RH11: Craw 6F 15
Amber Glade RH13: Southw 4B 36
Amberley Cl. RH10: Craw 5D 16
    RH12: Hors 3C 30
Amberley Ct. *RH11: Craw* *6G 9*
    (off County Oak La.)
    RH14: Bill 4H 37
Amberley Flds. Caravan Club Site
    RH11: Low H 5E 9
Amberley Rd. RH12: Hors 3C 30
Ambleside Cl. RH11: Ifield 6A 14
Amorosa Cl. RH11: Ifield 2D 14
Amundsen Rd. RH12: Hors 3H 29
Anaba Ho. RH11: Craw 6E 15
Anchor Cl. RH12: Hors 2G 33
Anderson Rd. RH10: Craw 3H 21
ANDREWS HILL 6E 37
Andrew's La. RH13: Southw 4B 36
Andrews Rd. RH13: Southw 6B 36
Andromeda Cl. RH11: Craw 1B 20
Angell Cl. RH10: Craw 6D 16
Anglesey Cl. RH11: Craw 2F 21
Angus Cl. RH12: Craw 5H 29
Ann Gream Ho. RH19: E Grin 3E 25
Antlands La. RH6: Ship B, Bur 3F 11
Antlands La. E. RH6: Ship B 3G 11
Antlands La. W. RH6: Ship B 3F 11
Anvil Cl. RH13: Southw 4B 36
    RH14: Bill 3F 37
Apperlie Dr. RH6: Horl 6H 5
Applefield RH10: Craw 4H 15
April Cl. RH12: Hors 5G 29
Apsley Ct. RH11: Craw 1C 20
Aquarius Ct. RH11: Craw 1B 20
Archers Ct. RH10: Craw 3G 15
Archway Theatre 5G 5
Arcturus Rd. RH11: Craw 2B 20
Arden Rd. RH10: Craw 1A 22
Ardingly Cl. RH11: Craw 3E 15
Argus Wlk. RH11: Craw 2D 20
Argyll Ct. *RH11: Craw* *6G 15*
    (off Perryfield Rd.)
Arkendale RH19: Felb 1A 24
Arne Ct. RH11: Craw 2C 20
Arne Gro. RH6: Horl 2D 4
Arnfield Cl. RH11: Ifield 6B 14
Arran Cl. RH11: Craw 2E 21
Arrancourt RH12: Hors 1E 33
Arrivals Rd. RH6: Gatw 1A 10
    (not continuous)
Artel Cft. RH10: Craw 5B 16
Arthur Rd. RH11: Ifield 5B 14
    RH13: Hors 2H 33
Arundel Ct. RH10: Craw 5D 16
    RH13: Southw 4C 36
Arundel Ct. *RH14: Bill* *4H 37*
    (off Brooker's Rd.)
Arundel Ho. *RH13: Hors* *2A 34*
    (off Kennedy Rd.)
Arun Gdns. RH13: Hors 2A 34
Arun Rd. RH14: Bill 2F 37
Arunside RH12: Hors 2E 33
Arun Way RH13: Hors 2A 34

Ashburnham Rd. RH10: Craw 1B 22
Ashby Ct. RH13: Hors 1A 34
Ash Cl. RH10: Craw D 3H 19
Ash Ct. RH19: E Grin 2E 25
Ashdown Cl. RH18: F Row 5G 27
    RH13: Hors 5B 30
Ashdown Dr. RH10: Craw 2G 21
Ashdown Ga. RH19: E Grin 3D 24
Ashdown Ho. RH6: Gatw 2B 10
Ashdown Rd. RH18: F Row 5F 27
Ashdown Vw. RH19: E Grin 6E 25
Ashington Ct. *RH12: Hors* *4H 29*
    (off Woodstock Cl.)
Ash Keys RH10: Craw 6H 15
Ashleigh Cl. RH6: Horl 4E 5
Ashleigh Rd. RH12: Hors 4G 29
Ashmore Ho. RH11: Craw 2G 15
Ash Rd. RH10: Craw 4B 16
    RH13: Southw 4A 36
Ashurst Cl. RH12: Hors 4C 30
Ashurst Dr. RH10: Worth 5E 17
ASHURST WOOD 1D 26
Ashwood RH11: Craw 6G 15
Ashwood Ct. RH18: F Row 6F 27
Aspen Ct. RH19: E Grin 5G 25
Aspen Way RH12: Hors 5A 30
Aston Ct. RH11: Craw 4E 21
Astral Towers RH10: Craw 1G 15
Athelstan Cl. RH10: Worth 5F 17
Athelstan Way RH13: Southw 3A 34
Atkinson Ct. RH6: Horl 5G 5
Atkinson Rd. RH10: Craw 1D 22
Atlantic Ho. RH6: Gatw 1B 10
Atrium, The 4E 25
Auchinleck Ct. RH10: Craw D 4G 19
Auckland Cl. RH11: Craw 6B 14
Aurum Cl. RH6: Horl 5G 5
Austen Ct. RH19: E Grin 4B 24
Autumn Cl. RH11: Craw 6F 15
Avebury Cl. RH12: Hors 2C 30
Aveling Cl. RH10: Craw 1D 22
Avenue, The RH6: Horl 5E 5
    RH10: Craw 4G 21
    RH13: Hors 5B 32
Avenue Gdns. RH6: Horl 5H 5
Aviary Way RH10: Craw D 2H 19
Avondale Cl. RH6: Horl 2E 5
Avon Wlk. RH11: Craw 6C 14
Ayshe Ct. Dr. RH13: Hors 1A 34

Baden Dr. RH6: Horl 3D 4
Bader Ct. RH10: Craw 3G 15
Badgers Cl. RH11: Craw 3B 30
Badger's Way RH19: E Grin 3F 25
Bailey Cl. RH12: Hors 2B 30
Bailing Hill RH12: Warnh 2C 28
Baird Cl. RH10: Craw 2B 16
Bakehouse Barn Cl. RH12: Hors 2A 30
Bakehouse Rd. RH6: Horl 2E 5
Baker Cl. RH10: Craw 1G 21
Bakers Ct. RH13: Southw 4B 36
Balcombe Ct. RH10: Craw 4E 17
Balcombe Gdns. RH6: Horl 5H 5
Balcombe La. RH17: Bal 6G 23
Balcombe Rd. RH6: Horl 3G 5
    RH10: Craw, Worth 4E 11
Baldwin Cl. RH10: Craw 2D 22
Baldwins Fld. RH19: E Grin 1D 24
BALDWINS HILL 1D 24
Balfour Gdns. RH18: F Row 6E 27
Balliol Cl. RH10: Craw 2D 16
Balmoral RH19: E Grin 5G 25
Balmoral Ct. RH11: Craw 3E 21
Bamborough Cl. RH13: Southw 4C 36
Bancroft Rd. RH10: Craw 6E 17
Bank La. RH10: Craw 5G 15
Bank Pct. RH10: Craw 2B 16
Banks Rd. RH10: Craw 5G 15
Barber Cl. RH10: Craw 3D 22
Barley Cl. RH10: Craw 6G 15
Barley Ho. *RH10: Craw* *6G 15*
    (off Barley Cl.)

Barleymead RH6: Horl 3G 5
Barlow Rd. RH11: Craw 2B 20
Barn Cl. RH10: Craw 5E 17
    RH11: Pease P 6E 21
Barnes Ho. *RH13: Hors* *6B 32*
    (off The Avenue)
Barnes M. RH13: Hors 1F 33
Barnes Wallis Av. RH13: Hors 5B 32
Barnfield RH6: Horl 5F 5
Barn Field Pl. RH19: E Grin 2G 25
Barnfield Rd. RH10: Craw 4G 15
Barnsnap Cl. RH12: Hors 3H 29
Barnwood RH10: Craw 4D 16
Barrackfield Wlk. RH12: Hors 3F 33
Barrington Rd. RH10: Craw 1G 21
    RH13: Hors 1A 34
Barrow Way RH14: Bill 4F 37
Barry Cl. RH10: Craw 2H 21
Bartholomew Way RH12: Hors 3C 30
Barton Cres. RH19: E Grin 5G 25
Barton Wlk. RH10: Craw 1C 22
Barttelot Rd. RH12: Hors 2H 33
Basepoint Bus. Cen. RH11: Craw 1G 15
Bashford Way RH10: Craw 3E 17
Basildon Way RH11: Craw 2B 20
Bassett Rd. RH10: Craw 2E 23
Bateman Ct. RH10: Craw 2B 22
Baxter Cl. RH10: Craw 1C 22
Bay Cl. RH6: Horl 1D 4
Bayfield Rd. RH6: Horl 3D 4
Bayhorne La. RH6: Horl 6H 5
Baylis Wlk. RH11: Craw 4E 21
Beachy Rd. RH11: Craw 4D 20
Beacon Ct. RH13: Hors 5C 30
Beacon Ri. RH19: E Grin 2H 25
Beale Ct. RH11: Craw 2D 20
Bearsden Way RH12: Broadb H 6B 28
Beaumont Cl. RH11: Ifield 6B 14
Beaver Cl. RH12: Hors 3A 30
Beckett La. RH11: Craw 2G 15
Beckett Way RH19: E Grin 5F 25
Beckford Way RH10: Craw 3C 22
Bedale Cl. RH11: Craw 1F 21
Bedford Rd. RH13: Hors 2H 33
Beech Cl. RH19: E Grin 3D 24
Beech Ct. RH19: E Grin 3D 24
Beeches Cres. RH10: Craw 1H 21
Beeches La. RH19: Ash W 1D 26
Beechey Cl. RH10: Copt 6A 12
Beechey Way RH10: Copt 6A 12
Beechfields RH19: E Grin 2F 25
Beech Gdns. RH10: Craw D 4F 19
Beech Holme RH10: Craw D 3G 19
Beech Ho. RH10: Craw 1G 15
Beeching Way RH19: E Grin 4E 25
Beech Rd. RH12: Hors 4D 30
Beechside RH10: Craw 6H 15
Beech Tree Cl. RH10: Craw 4G 15
Beechwood RH13: Southw 5B 36
Beeding Cl. RH12: Hors 4C 30
Beedingwood Dr. RH12: Colg 3G 31
Beehive Ring Rd. RH6: Craw 4C 10
Beggarhouse La. RH6: Charlw 1A 8
Behenna Cl. RH11: Craw 6B 14
Belgravia Ct. *RH6: Horl* *4G 5*
    (off St Georges Ct.)
Belinus Dr. RH14: Bill 3F 37
Bellamy Rd. RH10: Craw 3D 22
Bell Cen., The RH10: Craw 1A 16
Bell Hammer RH19: E Grin 5E 25
Belloc Cl. RH10: Craw 4C 16
Belloc Ct. RH13: Hors 6C 30
Bell Rd. RH12: Warnh 1D 28
Belvedere Ct. RH10: Craw 4C 16
Benchfield Cl. RH19: E Grin 5H 25
Benhams Cl. RH6: Horl 2F 5
Benhams Dr. RH6: Horl 2F 5
Benjamin Rd. RH10: Craw 1E 23
Bennett Cl. RH10: Craw 3C 22
Bennetts Rd. RH13: Hors 2A 34
Bens Acre RH13: Hors 1C 34
Bensons La. RH12: Fay 1E 31
Berkeley Cl. RH11: Craw 3A 20
Berrall Way RH14: Bill 4E 37
Berrymeade Wlk. RH11: Ifield 6B 14
Berstead Wlk. RH11: Craw 2C 20
Betchley Cl. RH19: E Grin 2E 25

Betchworth Works RH6: Charlw 3A 8
Bethune Cl. RH10: Worth 6E 17
Bethune Rd. RH13: Hors 2A 34
Betts Way RH10: Craw 1G 15
Beulah Cl. RH6: Horl 4F 5
Bevan Ct. RH11: Craw 4E 21
Beverley M. RH10: Craw 6B 16
BEWBUSH 2C 20
Bewbush Dr. RH11: Craw 2B 20
Bewbush Mnr. Rdbt. RH11: Craw 3B 20
Bewbush Pl. RH11: Craw 2B 20
Bewbush Water Garden 1A 20
Bickley Ct. RH11: Craw 2D 20
Biggin Cl. RH11: Craw 1F 21
Bignor Cl. RH12: Hors 3C 30
Bilberry Cl. RH11: Craw 2E 21
Bilbets RH12: Hors 6G 29
                                        (off North Pde.)
BILLINGSHURST 2G 37
Billingshurst Rd. RH12: Broadb H 6A 28
Billingshurst Station (Rail) 4G 37
Billington Ct. RH19: E Grin 3E 25
Billinton Dr. RH10: Craw 5C 16
Binney Ct. RH10: Craw 2F 17
Binstead Cl. RH11: Craw 3E 15
Birch Cl. RH10: Craw D 3H 19
Birch Dr. RH14: Bill 4G 37
Birches, The RH10: Craw 3B 16
   RH13: Mann H 4E 35
Birches Ind. Est. RH19: E Grin 2A 24
Birches Rd. RH12: Hors 4D 30
Birchfield Est. RH6: Charlw 5A 8
Birch Gro. RH19: Felb 6B 24
Birch Ho. RH19: E Grin 3C 24
Birch Lea RH10: Craw 2B 16
Birch Tree Gdns. RH19: E Grin 2B 24
Birchwood Cl. RH6: Horl 3G 5
   RH10: Craw 2D 22
Birdham Cl. RH11: Craw 3E 15
Birkdale Dr. RH11: Ifield 6A 14
Bisham Cl. RH10: Craw 1E 23
Bishopric RH12: Hors 1F 33
Bishopric RH12: Hors 1F 33
Bishops Ct. RH12: Hors 2G 33
Bishopstone Wlk. RH11: Craw 4F 21
Bitmead Cl. RH11: Ifield 6B 14
Bittern Cl. RH11: Ifield 6A 14
Blackbird Hill RH10: Turn H 6H 19
Blackbridge Ct. RH12: Hors 1F 33
Blackbridge La. RH12: Hors 2E 33
Blackcap Cl. RH11: Craw 1F 21
BLACK CORNER 4E 11
Black Dog Wlk. RH10: Craw 3H 15
Blackett Rd. RH10: Craw 6D 16
Blackfold Rd. RH10: Craw 6B 16
Blackheath RH10: Craw 3E 17
Blackhorse Way RH12: Hors 1F 33
Blacklands Cres. RH18: F Row 5F 27
Black Swan Cl. RH11: Pease P 6E 21
Blackthorn Cl. RH11: Craw 3F 15
   RH13: Hors 1C 34
Blackwater La. RH10: Craw 6D 16
BLACKWELL 3E 25
Blackwell Farm Rd. RH19: E Grin 2F 25
Blackwell Hollow RH19: E Grin 3F 25
Blackwell Rd. RH19: E Grin 3F 25
Blake Cl. RH10: Craw 3A 22
Blakes Farm Rd. RH13: Southw 6E 33
Blatchford Cl. RH13: Hors 6B 30
Blatchford Rd. RH13: Hors 6B 30
Blenheim Cl. RH10: Craw 2E 17
   RH19: E Grin .2G 25
Blenheim Flds. RH18: F Row 4E 27
Blenheim Rd. RH12: Hors 4H 29
Bligh Cl. RH10: Craw 1A 22
Blindley Rd. RH10: Craw 2E 17
Bloor Cl. RH12: Hors 2H 29
Blount Av. RH19: E Grin 4C 24
Bluebell Cl. RH11: Craw 2E 21
   RH12: Hors 4A 30
   RH19: E Grin .4B 24
Bluecoat Pond RH13: Hors 5B 32
Bluecoat Sports Health & Fitness Club
                                             . . . . .5B 32
Blundell Av. RH6: Horl 3E 5
Blunts Way RH12: Hors 6G 29
Blytons, The RH19: E Grin 4B 24

Bodiam Cl. RH10: Craw 5D 16
   RH13: Southw 3C 36
Boleyn Cl. RH10: Craw 2E 23
Bolney Ct. RH11: Craw 2C 20
Bolters Rd. RH6: Horl 2F 5
Bolters Rd. Sth. RH6: Horl 2E 5
Bolton Rd. RH10: Craw 4C 22
Bonehurst Rd. RH1: Salf 1F 5
   RH6: Horl 1F 5
Bonfire Hill RH13: Southw 4A 36
Bonnetts La. RH11: Ifield 1D 14
Bonwicke Cotts. RH10: Copt 3B 12
Booth Rd. RH11: Craw 2B 20
Booth Way RH13: Hors 6A 30
Borage Cl. RH11: Craw 2D 20
Border Chase RH10: Copt 1H 17
Border Ct. RH19: E Grin 1F 25
Borers Arms Rd. RH10: Copt 5A 12
Borers Cl. RH10: Copt 5B 12
Borers Yd. Ind. Est. RH10: Copt 6B 12
Borrowdale Cl. RH11: Craw 1E 21
Bosham Rd. RH10: Craw 2D 22
Bostock Av. RH12: Hors 1A 34
Boswell Rd. RH10: Craw 2H 21
Bottings Hill RH13: Southw 5C 36
Boulevard, The RH10: Craw 5G 15
                                             (not continuous)
Boundary Cl. RH10: Craw 4H 15
Boundary Rd. RH10: Craw 4H 15
Bourg-de-Peage Av. RH19: E Grin 4G 25
Bourne Ct. RH13: Hors 6A 30
Bowater Rd. RH10: Craw 2D 22
Bower, The RH10: Craw 6D 16
Bowers Pl. RH10: Craw D 3G 19
Bowes Cl. RH13: Hors 6A 30
Bowling Grn. La. RH12: Hors 6H 29
Bowman Ct. RH10: Craw 4G 15
                                             (off London Rd.)
Bowness Cl. RH11: Ifield 6A 14
Boxall Wlk. RH13: Hors 2H 33
Box Cl. RH11: Craw 4F 21
Box La. RH19: Ash W 1E 27
Bracken Cl. RH10: Copt 6A 12
   RH10: Craw 3H 15
Bracken Gro. RH12: Hors 4D 30
Brackenside RH6: Horl 3G 5
Bracklyn Av. RH19: Felb 4H 13
Bracknell Wlk. RH11: Craw 3B 20
Bradbury Rd. RH10: Craw 2D 22
Braeburn Cl. RH11: Ifield 2D 14
Bramber Cl. RH10: Craw 3H 15
   RH12: Hors 4D 30
Bramber Ho. RH13: Hors 2A 34
                                             (off Kennedy Rd.)
Bramble Cl. RH10: Copt 6A 12
Bramble Twitten RH19: E Grin 4G 25
Brambletye La. RH18: F Row 3D 26
Brambletye Rd. RH10: Craw 6B 16
Brambling Ct. RH13: Hors 2C 34
Brambling Rd. RH13: Hors 2C 34
Bramley Cl. RH10: Craw 5A 16
Bramley Wlk. RH6: Horl 4H 5
Brandon Cl. RH10: Craw 1E 23
Brantridge Rd. RH10: Craw 1A 22
Bray Cl. RH10: Craw 1E 23
Breezehurst Dr. RH11: Craw 2B 20
Breezehurst Rdbt. RH11: Craw 3D 20
Bremner Av. RH6: Horl 3E 5
Brettingham Cl. RH11: Craw 2B 20
Brewer Rd. RH10: Craw 1H 21
Breydon Wlk. RH10: Craw 1C 22
Briar Cl. RH11: Craw 2F 15
Briars Wood RH6: Horl 3H 5
Briarswood Cl. RH10: Craw 3E 17
Brickfield La. RH6: Hookw 6C 4
Bricklands RH10: Craw D 4G 19
Brickyard La. RH10: Craw D 3G 19
Brideake Cl. RH11: Craw 2D 20
Bridgeham Way RH6: Smallf 5E 7
Bridge Ind. Est. RH6: Horl 4G 5
Bridgelands RH10: Copt 6H 11
Bridges Cl. RH6: Horl 4A 6
Bridges Ct. RH12: Hors 4B 30
Bridges Pl. RH12: Hors 2G 33
Bridgestone Pl. RH13: Hors 2A 34
Bridgewater Cl. RH14: Bill 5F 37
Bridle Way RH10: Craw 4E 17

Brighton Rd. RH6: Gatw, Craw 6E 5
   RH6: Horl 5E 5
   RH10: Craw 2G 21
   RH11: Craw 5F 21
   RH11: Pease P 6F 21
   RH13: Hors, Mann H, Lwr Bee, Monks G
                                             . . . . .2H 33
Brisbane Cl. RH11: Craw 2G 15
Bristol Cl. RH10: Craw 2E 17
British Rail New Yd. RH10: Craw 1C 16
Britten Cl. RH11: Craw 2C 20
   RH13: Hors 5D 30
BROADBRIDGE 6D 6
Broadbridge Cotts. RH6: Smallf 6D 6
BROADBRIDGE HEATH 6B 28
Broadbridge Heath By-Pass
   RH12: Broadb H 6A 28
Broadbridge Heath Leisure Cen. 1B 32
Broadbridge Heath Rd.
   RH12: Broadb H, Warnh 5B 28
Broadbridge La. RH6: Smallf 4D 6
Broadbridge Retail Pk.
   RH12: Broadb H 6C 28
BROADFIELD 3E 21
Broadfield Barton RH11: Craw 3E 21
Broadfield Dr. RH11: Craw 2E 21
Broadfield Park 4F 21
Broadfield Pk. RH11: Craw 3G 21
Broadfield Pl. RH11: Craw 3E 21
Broadfield Rdbt. RH11: Craw 2E 21
Broadfield Stadium 3F 21
Broadlands RH6: Horl 3H 5
Broadmead RH6: Horl 3H 5
Broadstone RH18: F Row 5G 15
Broadwalk RH10: Craw 5G 15
Broadway, The RH10: Craw 5G 15
Broadwood Cl. RH12: Hors 4C 30
Broadwood Ri. RH11: Craw 4D 20
Brockham Keep RH6: Horl 3H 5
                                             (off Langshott La.)
Brockhurst Cl. RH12: Hors 2D 32
Brock Rd. RH11: Craw 2E 15
Brontes, The RH19: E Grin 4D 24
Brook, The RH10: Craw 4G 15
   RH13: Southw 3C 36
Brook Cl. RH11: Craw 4H 25
Brooker's Rd. RH14: Bill 4G 37
Brookfield Dr. RH6: Horl 2G 5
Brookfield Way RH14: Bill 5G 37
Brookhill Cl. RH10: Copt 6H 11
Brookhill Rd. RH10: Copt 1H 17
Brooklands Rd. RH11: Craw 4F 21
Brooklands Way RH19: E Grin 5D 24
Brook La. RH12: Fay 1E 31
Brook Rd. RH12: Hors 3A 30
Brookside RH10: Copt 6H 11
   RH10: Craw 4A 16
   RH10: Craw D 3G 19
Brookview RH10: Copt 6H 11
Brookwood RH6: Horl 3G 5
Brookwood Ho. RH6: Horl 1G 4
                                             (off Skipton Way
Brookwood Pk. RH6: Horl 5G
Broomdashers Rd. RH10: Craw 4A 16
Broome Cl. RH12: Hors 4H 29
Broomfield Dr. RH14: Bill 4H 37
Broomwicks Pl. RH12: Broadb H 6C 28
                                             (off Sullington Mead)
Browning Cl. RH10: Craw 4D 16
Brownings, The RH19: E Grin 4C 24
Brownjohn Ct. RH10: Craw 4B 16
Browns Wood RH19: E Grin 1E 25
Brunel Cen., The RH10: Craw 1A 22
Brunel Pl. RH10: Craw 6H 15
Brunswick Cl. RH10: Craw 1B 22
Brunswick Ct. RH10: Craw 1B 22
                                             (off Brunswick Cl.)
Brushwood Rd. RH12: Hors 3D 33
Bryce Cl. RH12: Hors 4C 30
Buchan Country Pk. 3B 20
Buchan Country Pk. Countryside Cen.
                                             . . . . .3C 21
BUCHAN HILL 5D 20
Buchan Pk. RH11: Craw 3C 20
Buchans Lawn RH11: Craw 3E 21
Buckhurst Cl. RH19: E Grin 2C 24
Buckhurst Mead RH19: E Grin 1C 24

Buckhurst Way RH19: E Grin 2C 24
Buckingham Ct. RH11: Craw 3E 21
Buckingham Dr. RH19: E Grin 5G 25
Buckingham Ga. RH6: Gatw 2D 10
Buckley La. RH13: Hors, Mann H 5B 34
Buckley Pl. RH10: Craw D 3F 19
Buckmans Rd. RH11: Craw 4G 15
Buckshead Hill RH13: Plum P 4H 35
Buckswood Dr. RH11: Craw 1D 20
Budgen Cl. RH10: Craw 2E 17
Bullfinch Cl. RH6: Horl 3D 4
RH12: Hors 2G 29
Bulrushes Farm RH19: E Grin 6D 24
Bunting Cl. RH13: Hors 6B 30
Bunyan Cl. RH11: Craw 2B 20
Burbeach Cl. RH11: Craw 2E 21
Burdett Cl. RH10: Worth 6E 17
Burdock Cl. RH11: Craw 3D 20
Burford Rd. RH13: Hors 1A 34
Burgh Cl. RH10: Craw 2E 17
Burlands RH11: Craw 2D 14
Burleigh Cl. RH10: Craw D 3G 19
Burleigh La. RH10: Craw D 4G 19
Burleigh Way RH10: Craw D 4G 19
Burleys Rd. RH11: Craw 5D 16
Burney Ct. RH11: Craw 2D 20
Burnham Pl. RH13: Hors 2H 33
Burns Cl. RH12: Hors 2A 30
Burns Rd. RH10: Craw 3D 16
Burns Way RH12: Fay 4A 20
RH19: E Grin 4C 24
Burrell Ct. RH11: Craw 1C 20
Burston Gdns. RH19: E Grin 1D 24
BURSTOW 2H 11
Burstow Ent. Pk. RH6: Smallf 2B 12
Burstow Golf Course 4H 11
Burstow Lodge Bus. Cen. RH6: Smallf . . .2E 7
Burstow Pk. Bus. Cen. RH6: Ship B . . .4H 11
Burton Cl. RH6: Horl 5F 5
Burtons Ct. RH12: Hors 1G 33
Burwash Rd. RH10: Craw 6B 16
Bush La. RH12: Hors 1C 30
Butlers Rd. RH13: Hors 5C 30
Buttercup Way RH13: Southw 3C 36
Butterfield RH19: E Grin 2B 24
Buttermere Cl. RH12: Hors 3D 30
Buttermere Ct. *RH10: Craw* 1E 23
(off Grayrigg Rd.)
Butts Cl. RH11: Craw 4E 15
Bycroft Way RH10: Craw 3C 16
Byerley Way RH11: Craw 4E 17
Byfleets La. RH12: Broadb H, Warnh . . .3B 28
Byrd Rd. RH11: Craw 2C 20
RH12: Hors 3A 30
Byron Gro. RH19: E Grin 5C 24

C

Caburn Ct. RH11: Craw 1F 21
Caburn Hgts. RH11: Craw 1F 21
Cackstones, The RH10: Craw 3E 17
Caffins Ct. RH10: Craw 3H 15
Caffyns Ri. RH14: Bill 2G 37
Caldbeck Ho. *RH11: Craw* 2C 20
(off Salvington Rd.)
Calderdale Cl. RH11: Craw 1E 21
Caledonian Ho. *RH10: Craw* 3G 15
(off Barnfield Rd.)
Caledonian Way RH6: Gatw 2C 10
Callisto Cl. RH11: Craw 2B 20
Calluna Dr. RH10: Copt 1H 17
Calvin Wlk. RH11: Craw 2B 20
Camber Cl. RH10: Craw 5D 16
Cambridge Lodge Pk. RH6: Horl 1F 5
Cambridge Rd. RH13: Hors 1H 33
Camelot Cl. RH13: Southw 3C 36
Camelot Ct. RH11: Ifield 5B 14
Campbell Cres. RH19: E Grin 4B 24
Campbell Rd. RH10: Craw 1D 22
Campion Rd. RH12: Hors 4A 30
Canberra Cl. RH11: Craw 2G 15
Canberra Pl. RH12: Hors 5B 30
Cansiron La. RH19: Ash W 1F 27
Cantelupe Ho. *RH19: E Grin* 4F 25
(off Cantelupe Rd.)

Cantelupe M. *RH19: E Grin* 4F 25
(off Cantelupe Rd.)
Cantelupe Rd. RH19: E Grin 4F 25
Canter, The RH10: Craw 4F 17
Canterbury Ct. *RH13: Southw* 3C 36
(off Porchester Cl.)
Canterbury Rd. RH10: Craw 3H 21
Canvey Cl. RH11: Craw 2F 21
Capel La. RH11: Craw 6C 14
Capitol, The .1H 33
Capricorn Cl. RH11: Craw 1B 20
Capsey Rd. RH11: Ifield 5B 14
Captains Wlk. RH11: Craw 1F 21
Capua Ct. RH10: Craw 1D 16
Caraway Cl. RH11: Craw 3E 21
Card Hill RH18: F Row 6F 27
Carey Ho. RH11: Craw 5F 15
Careys Cl. RH6: Smallf 3E 7
Careys Copse RH6: Smallf 4E 7
Carey's Wood RH6: Smallf 4E 7
Carfax RH12: Hors 1G 33
Cargo Forecourt Rd.
RH6: Gatw 2G 9
Cargo Rd. RH6: Gatw 1G 9
Carlton Cl. RH10: Craw 6H 15
Carlton Ct. RH6: Horl 2F 5
Carlton Tye RH6: Horl 4H 5
Carman Wlk. RH11: Craw 4E 21
Caroline Ct. RH11: Craw 6G 15
Carpenters RH14: Bill 3G 37
Carrier Bus. Pk. RH10: Craw 4C 16
Carter Rd. RH10: Craw 2E 23
Cartersmead Cl. RH6: Horl 3G 5
Carylls Cotts. RH12: Fay 1H 31
Casher Rd. RH10: Craw 2D 22
Castle, The RH12: Hors 2A 30
Castle Dr. RH6: Horl 6H 5
Castlerigg Way RH10: Craw 1E 23
Castle Rd. RH12: Broadb H 6B 28
Castlewood Rd. RH13: Southw 3C 36
Caterways RH12: Hors 6E 29
Causeway RH12: Hors 2G 33
Cavalier Way RH19: E Grin 6F 25
Cavell Way RH10: Craw 6D 16
Cavendish Cl. RH12: Hors 2H 29
Caxton Cl. RH10: Craw 2G 21
Cedar Cl. RH11: Craw 2F 15
RH12: Hors 6F 29
Cedar Dr. RH13: Southw 3B 36
Cedar Lodge RH11: Craw 1G 21
Cedars, The RH14: Bill 4F 37
Cedars Farm RH14: Bill 3F 37
Celandine Cl. RH11: Craw 2E 21
Central Pde. RH6: Horl 5F 5
Chadwick Cl. RH11: Craw 4E 21
Chaffinch Cl. RH11: Craw 3G 15
RH12: Hors 2H 29
Chaffinch Way RH6: Horl 3D 4
Chailey Cl. RH11: Craw 2D 20
Chaldon Rd. RH11: Craw 4F 21
Challen Ct. RH11: Craw 6F 29
Chalmers Cl. RH6: Charlw 3B 8
Chanctonbury Way
RH11: Craw 1F 21
Chandler Cl. RH10: Craw 1G 21
Chandler Cl. RH6: Horl 4G 5
Chantlers Cl. RH19: E Grin 3C 24
Chantrey Rd. RH10: Craw 2H 21
Chantry Cl. RH6: Horl 3E 5
Chapel La. RH10: Craw D 6E 13
RH18: F Row 6F 27
RH19: Ash W 1D 26
Chapel Rd. RH6: Charlw 2B 8
RH6: Smallf 4E 7
Chapman Rd. RH10: Craw 3D 22
Chapman's La. RH19: E Grin 4B 24
(not continuous)
Charlesfield Rd. RH10: Horl 3E 5
Charleston Ct. RH10: Craw 2C 22
Charlock Cl. RH11: Craw 3D 20
Charlock Way RH11: Craw 3C 36
Charlotte Ct. *RH11: Craw* 5F 15
(off Leopold Rd.)
Charlotte Gro. RH6: Smallf 3D 6
CHARLWOOD 2B 8
Charlwood Cl. RH10: Copt 5H 11
Charlwood M. RH6: Charlw 2B 8

Charlwood Rd. RH6: Gatw 1F 9
RH11: Gatw, Low H 5E 9
RH11: Ifield 6B 8
Charlwoods Bus. Cen. RH19: E Grin 2D 24
Charlwoods Pl. RH19: E Grin 2E 25
Charlwoods Rd. RH19: E Grin 1E 25
Charlwood Wlk. RH11: Craw 2E 15
Charmans Cl. RH12: Hors 4D 30
Charm Cl. RH6: Horl 3D 4
Charrington Way RH12: Broadb H 6A 28
Chart Way RH12: Hors 1G 33
Chase, The RH10: Craw 6B 16
Chatelet Cl. RH6: Horl 3G 5
Chatfields RH11: Craw 1E 21
Chaucer Av. RH19: E Grin 5C 24
Chaucer Rd. RH10: Craw 3C 16
Cheals Rdbt. RH11: Craw 1E 21
Chelwood Cl. RH10: Craw 1A 22
Chennells Brook Cotts. *RH12: Hors* 2B 30
(off Giblets La.)
Chennells Way RH12: Hors 4H 29
Chepstow Cl. RH10: Craw 5F 17
Chequer Grange RH18: F Row 6E 27
Chequer Mead Theatre & Arts Cen. 4F 25
Chequer Rd. RH19: E Grin 4F 25
Chequers Cl. RH6: Horl 3F 5
Chequers Ct. RH13: Hors 6A 30
Chequers Dr. RH6: Horl 3F 5
Cherry Cl. RH13: Hors 2H 33
Cherry La. RH11: Craw 2F 15
Cherry Tree Cl. RH10: Craw 3E 17
RH14: Bill 2F 37
Cherry Tree Wlk. RH12: Hors 3D 30
Cherry Way RH19: Felb 6B 24
Cherwell Wlk. RH11: Craw 6C 14
Chesterfield Cl. RH19: Felb 5H 13
Chesters RH6: Horl 2D 4
Chesterton Cl. RH19: E Grin 6F 25
Chesterton Ct. RH13: Hors 5C 30
Chestnut Cl. RH19: E Grin 4G 25
Chestnut Ct. RH13: Hors 1A 34
Chestnut Gdns. RH12: Hors 4G 29
Chestnut Rd. RH6: Horl 2G 5
RH14: Bill 4G 37
Chestnuts, The RH6: Horl 2G 5
Chestnut Wlk. RH11: Craw 2F 15
Chesworth Cl. RH13: Hors 3G 33
Chesworth Cres. RH13: Hors 2G 33
Chesworth Gdns. RH13: Hors 2G 33
Chesworth La. RH13: Hors 2G 33
Chetnole RH19: E Grin 3D 24
Chetwood Rd. RH11: Craw 3A 20
Chevening Cl. RH11: Craw 4F 21
Cheviot Wlk. RH11: Craw 5E 15
Cheynell Wlk. RH11: Craw 1C 20
Cheyne Wlk. RH6: Horl 6E 5
Chichester Cl. RH10: Craw 3H 21
Chichester Ter. RH12: Hors 1H 33
Chiddingly Cl. RH10: Craw 6B 16
Chiltern Cl. RH11: Craw 5E 15
Chiltington Ct. *RH12: Hors* 5H 29
(off Blenheim Rd.)
Chippendale Rd. RH11: Craw 4B 16
Chithurst La. RH6: Horne . . . . . . .4H 7 & 2E 13
Choda Ho. RH10: Craw 6A 16
Christies RH19: E Grin 5D 24
Christopher Rd. RH19: E Grin 4E 25
Christ's Hospital Rd. RH13: Hors 5B 32
RH13: Itch 5A 32
Christs Hospital Station (Rail) 4B 32
Churchill Av. RH12: Hors 6F 29
Churchill Ct. RH10: Craw 2B 16
Churchill Rd. RH6: Smallf 4E 7
Church La. RH6: Bur 2G 11
RH6: Horl .3F 11
RH10: Copt 1H 17
RH10: Craw 4A 16
RH12: Broadb H 6B 28
RH13: Plum P, Lwr Bee 5H 35
RH13: Southw 4A 36
RH19: E Grin 4F 25
Church Pk. RH11: Low H 4H 9
Church Rd. RH6: Bur, Ship B, Smallf 2H 11
RH6: Horl .5E 5
RH6: Horne 1H 7
RH10: Copt 6A 12
RH10: Worth 5F 17

Church Rd. RH11: Low H 4H 9
RH12: Broadb H 6B 28
RH12: Hors 4D 30
RH13: Mann H 6E 35
Church Rd. Ind. Est. RH11: Low H 4A 10
Church St. RH10: Craw 5F 15
RH12: Warnh 2D 28
Church Vw. Cl. RH6: Horl 5E 5
Church Wlk. RH6: Horl 5E 5
RH10: Craw 5G 15
Cineworld Cinema
Crawley 4G 15
Cissbury Cl. RH12: Hors 3C 30
Cissbury Hill RH11: Craw 1F 21
City Bus. Cen. RH13: Hors 2H 33
City Bus. Centre, The RH11: Craw . . .1G 15
City Pl. RH6: Craw 4C 10
Clappers Ga. RH10: Craw 4G 15
Clare Cl. RH10: Craw 2D 16
Clarence Ct. RH6: Horl 3A 6
Clarence Dr. RH19: E Grin 6F 25
Clarence Rd. RH13: Hors 2H 33
Clarence Way RH6: Horl 3A 6
Clarke Ho. RH10: Craw 3B 16
Clark Rd. RH11: Craw 4D 20
Clay Hall La. RH10: Copt 5B 12
Clays Cl. RH19: E Grin 5E 25
Clayton Hill RH11: Craw 1F 21
Clevelands RH14: Bill 3G 37
Cleve Way RH14: Bill 3G 37
Clifton Cl. RH6: Horl 4A 6
Clifton Rd. RH10: Craw 6D 16
Climping Rd. RH11: Craw 3E 15
Clitherow Gdns. RH10: Craw 6H 15
Clive Way RH10: Craw 5D 16
Close, The RH6: Horl 6H 5
RH19: E Grin 5D 24
Cloverfields RH6: Horl 3G 5
Cloverlands RH10: Craw 3A 16
Clovers End RH12: Hors 4C 30
Clovers Way RH12: Fay 2F 31
Clover Way RH6: Smallf 4F 7
Coachman's Dr. RH11: Craw 3E 21
Coach Rd. RH6: Gatw 1A 10
Cobbett Cl. RH10: Craw 3D 16
Cobbles Cres. RH10: Craw 4H 15
Cob Cl. RH10: Craw D 3H 19
Cobham Way RH10: Craw 5C 10
Cobnor Cl. RH11: Craw 1C 20
Coburn Ho. RH10: Craw 4C 16
(off Trafalgar Gdns.)
Cob Wlk. RH11: Craw 5D 14
Cogmans La RH6: Out, Smallf 2G 7
Cogmans La. RH1: Out 2G 7
Colchester Va. RH18: F Row 5E 27
Cole Cl. RH11: Craw 4E 21
Coleridge Cl. RH12: Hors 3A 30
Coleridge Ho. RH13: Hors 6B 32
(off The Avenue)
Colet Rd. RH10: Craw 2G 21
Colgate Cl. RH11: Craw 3E 15
College Cl. RH19: E Grin 4F 25
College La. RH19: E Grin 4F 25
College Rd. RH10: Craw 5H 15
RH13: Southw 4A 36
Colletts All. RH12: Hors 1G 33
(off Middle St.)
Collier Row RH10: Craw 1G 21
Collingwood Cl. RH6: Horl 3G 5
RH12: Hors 5G 29
RH19: E Grin 6F 25
Collingwood Rd. RH10: Craw 6E 17
RH12: Hors 4F 29
Collins Rd. RH11: Craw 1B 20
Colne Wlk. RH11: Craw 1C 20
Colonsay Rd. RH11: Craw 2E 21
Coltash Rd. RH10: Craw 6B 16
Coltsfoot Dr. RH12: Hors 4A 30
Colwyn Cl. RH11: Craw 1C 20
Comfrey Ct. RH6: Horl 2H 5
(off Newman Rd.)
COMMON, THE 5G 29
Commonwealth Dr. RH10: Craw 5A 16
Compassion Cl. RH11: Craw 6B 14
Comper Cl. RH11: Craw 1B 20
Comptons, The RH11: Craw 6B 30
Comptons Brow La. RH13: Hors 6C 30

Comptons Ct. RH13: Hors 6B 30
Comptons La. RH13: Hors 5B 30
Coney Cl. RH11: Craw 3E 15
Coney Cft. RH12: Hors 4D 30
Conifers Cl. RH12: Hors 3D 30
Coniston Cl. RH11: Ifield 1A 20
RH12: Hors 4D 30
Connaught Gdns. RH10: Craw 3G 15
Consort Ho. RH6: Horl 4F 5
Consort Way RH6: Horl 4F 5
Consort Way E. RH6: Horl 5G 5
Constable Rd. RH10: Craw 3A 22
Control Twr. Rd. RH6: Gatw 3G 9
(not continuous)
Cook Rd. RH10: Craw 1H 21
RH12: Hors 3H 29
Coolham Ct. RH11: Ifield 5C 14
COOLHURST 3D 34
Coolhurst La. RH13: Hors 2C 34
Coombe Cl. RH11: Craw 2G 15
Coombe Hall Pk. RH19: E Grin 6D 24
Coombe Hill RH14: Bill 2G 37
Coombe Hill Rd. RH19: E Grin 6D 24
Cooper Cl. RH6: Smallf 4D 6
Cooper Row RH10: Craw 2G 21
Cootes Av. RH12: Hors 6E 29
Copeland Ho. RH11: Craw 2F 21
Copnall Way RH12: Hors 1G 33
Copperfield Pl. RH12: Hors 5F 29
Copperfields RH13: Hors 3D 34
Copperfields Mnr. RH13: Hors 3D 34
Coppice, The RH10: Craw D 3G 19
Coppice Rd. RH12: Hors 4C 30
Coppice Wlk. RH10: Craw 4B 16
Copse, The RH10: Craw 5B 16
(off Gales Dr.)
RH13: Southw 3B 36
Copse Cl. RH10: Craw D 3G 19
RH12: Hors 3B 30
RH19: E Grin 2G 25
Copse Cres. RH11: Craw 4F 15
Copse La. RH6: Horl 3H 5
COPTHORNE 6H 11
Copthorne Bank RH10: Copt 3B 12
COPTHORNE COMMON 6C 12
Copthorne Comn. Rd.
RH10: Copt 1H 17
Copthorne Golf Course 6B 12
Copthorne Rd. RH10: Copt 5G 13
RH10: Craw 3E 17
RH19: Copt, Felb . . . . . .5G 13 & 6A 24
Copthorne Way RH10: Craw 1F 17
Copyhold Rd. RH19: E Grin 5D 24
Corby Cl. RH11: Craw 2B 20
Corfe Cl. RH13: Southw 4C 36
Cornflower Way RH13: Southw 2C 36
Cornwall Gdns. RH19: E Grin 5F 25
Coronation Rd. RH19: E Grin 6E 25
Coronet, The RH6: Horl 6H 5
Coronet Cl. RH10: Craw 4F 17
Corsletts Av. RH12: Broadb H 6B 28
Corunna Dr. RH13: Hors 1B 34
Cotsford RH11: Pease P 6E 21
Cotswold Cl. RH11: Craw 5E 15
Cotswold Ct. RH13: Hors 1A 34
Cottage Cl. RH12: Hors 3D 30
Cottage Pl. RH10: Copt 6D 12
Cottesmore Golf Course 6B 20
Cottingham Av. RH12: Hors 2H 29
Cotton Wlk. RH11: Craw 4D 20
County Bldgs. RH10: Craw 5H 15
County Court
Horsham 6G 29
County Mall Shop. Cen.
RH10: Craw 5H 15
COUNTY OAK 1G 15
County Oak La. RH11: Craw 1G 15
County Oak Retail Pk. RH11: Craw 1G 15
County Oak Way RH11: Craw 1G 15
Court Cl. RH19: E Grin 4F 25
Court Cres. RH19: E Grin 4F 25
Court Lodge Rd. RH6: Horl 3D 4
Courtoak La. RH1: Out 2E 7
Courtyard, The RH10: Craw 6G 15
RH12: Hors 1G 33
RH13: Colg 5G 31
RH19: E Grin 4H 25

Coverdale Ct. RH19: E Grin 2C 24
Covert Cl. RH10: Craw 4H 15
Covey, The RH10: Craw 3E 17
Cowdray Cl. RH10: Craw 6D 16
Cowfold Cl. RH11: Craw 2C 20
Cowslip Cl. RH13: Southw 2C 36
Coxcomb Wlk. RH11: Craw 1C 20
Cox Ho. RH12: Hors 1F 33
CRABBET PARK 4F 17
Crabbet Pk. RH10: Worth 4G 17
Crabbet Rd. RH10: Craw 4C 16
Crabtree Ct. RH11: Craw 4F 15
Crabtree Rd. RH11: Craw 4F 15
Craigans RH11: Craw 5D 14
Cranborne Wlk. RH10: Craw 1A 22
Cranbourne Cl. RH6: Horl 2G 5
Cranham Av. RH14: Bill 5F 37
Cranmer Wlk. RH10: Craw 6D 16
Cranston Gdns. RH19: E Grin 3E 25
Cranston Rd. RH19: E Grin 3E 25
Cranston Way RH10: Craw D 3H 19
Craven Ct. RH19: E Grin 3F 25
(off Badger's Way)
Craven Rd. RH10: Craw 6C 16
Cravens, The RH6: Smallf 4D 6
Crawford Gdns. RH13: Hors 5A 30
Crawfurd Way RH19: E Grin 3E 25
CRAWLEY .5G 15
Crawley Av. RH10: Craw 3H 15
RH11: Craw 4E 15
Crawley Bus. Quarter
RH10: Craw 1H 15
CRAWLEY DOWN 4G 19
Crawley Down Rd. RH19: Felb 6A 24
Crawley Foyer RH11: Craw 5F 15
Crawley Goods Yd. RH10: Craw 6C 10
CRAWLEY HOSPITAL 5F 15
Crawley La. RH10: Craw 4D 16
Crawley Lawn Tennis Club 3C 16
Crawley Leisure Pk. RH10: Craw 4G 15
Crawley Museum Cen. 6F 15
Crawley Rd. RH12: Fay 3A 20
RH12: Hors, Fay . . . . . .5B 30 & 3A 20
Crawley Sth. West By-Pass
RH11: Pease P 3B 20
Crawley Station (Rail) 6H 15
Crawley Town FC 3F 21
Crawters Cl. RH10: Craw 4D 16
Creasys Dr. RH11: Craw 4D 20
Crescent, The RH6: Horl 6F 5
RH12: Hors 2E 33
Crescent Ct. RH6: Horl 6F 5
Crescent Rd. RH19: E Grin 4D 24
Crescent Way RH6: Horl 6F 5
Crewdson Rd. RH6: Horl 4G 5
Cricket Ct. RH19: E Grin 2E 25
Cricketfield Rd. RH12: Hors 2F 33
Cripplegate La. RH13: Southw 5C 36
Cripps Ho. RH11: Craw 3E 21
Crockham Cl. RH11: Craw 1F 21
Crockhurst RH13: Southw 3C 36
Croft, The RH11: Craw 5D 14
Croft Way RH12: Hors 6E 29
Crompton Flds. RH10: Craw 2H 15
Crompton Way RH10: Craw 3H 15
Cromwell Pl. RH19: E Grin 6F 25
Cross Keys RH10: Craw 5G 11
Cross La. RH6: Smallf 1B 12
Crossman Ct. RH11: Craw 4D 21
Crosspath RH10: Craw 4H 15
Crossway RH6: Gatw 1A 10
Crossways RH10: Craw 4A 16
Crossways Av. RH19: E Grin 4A 16
Crossways Cl. RH10: Craw 4A 16
Crowberry Cl. RH11: Craw 3D 20
Crowhurst Cl. RH10: Worth 5F 17
Crowhurst Keep RH10: Worth 5F 17
Crown All. RH12: Hors 1G 33
(off Carfa...)
Crutchfield La. RH6: Sid . . . . .1A...
Cuckfield Cl. RH11: Craw . . . . .2C 2...
Cuckmere Cres. RH11: Craw . . . . .6C 1...
Cumbernauld Wlk.
RH11: Craw . . . . .3B 2...
Curteys Wlk. RH11: Craw . . . . .2C 2...
Curzon Av. RH12: Hors . . . . .6F 2...
Cuttinglye La. RH10: Craw D . . . . .2F 1...

Cuttinglye Rd. RH10: Craw D 1G 19
CUTTINGLYE WOOD 1H 19

D

Dairyfields RH11: Craw 6D 14
Dakin Cl. RH10: Craw 3D 22
Dakins, The RH19: E Grin 5E 25
Dale Cl. RH12: Hors 4B 30
Daledene RH19: E Grin 5F 25
(off Lewes Rd.)
Dale Rd. RH18: F Row 6F 27
Dalewood Gdns. RH10: Craw 3A 16
Dallaway Gdns. RH19: E Grin 4E 25
Dalton Cl. RH11: Craw 4D 20
Dampier Wlk. RH11: Craw 4E 21
Danby Ct. RH6: Horl 2F 5
Danehurst Cres. RH13: Hors 1B 34
Daniels Ho. RH10: Craw 4C 16
(off Trafalgar Gdns.)
Darenth Way RH6: Horl 2E 5
Darleydale RH11: Craw 2F 21
Dart Ct. RH19: E Grin 2G 25
Darwin Cl. RH12: Hors 5B 30
Daux Av. RH14: Bill 5G 37
Daux Hill RH12: Warnh 2F 29
Daux Rd. RH14: Bill 4G 37
Daux Rd. Ind. Est. RH14: Bill 4G 37
Daux Way RH14: Bill 5G 37
Dauxwood Cl. RH14: Bill 5G 37
Davis Cl. RH11: Craw 4D 20
Dawn Rd. RH10: Copt 6H 11
Dedisham Cl. RH10: Craw 6B 16
Deepfields RH6: Horl 2E 5
Deerhurst Pk. RH18: F Row 5G 27
Deerswood Cl. RH11: Craw 4E 15
Deerswood Ct. RH11: Craw 4D 14
Deerswood Rd. RH11: Craw 5E 15
Deer Way RH12: Hors 2E 33
Delancey Ct. RH12: Hors 5G 29
(off Wimblehurst Rd.)
De La Warr Rd. RH19: E Grin 4F 25
Delfont Cl. RH10: Craw 1E 23
Delius Gdns. RH13: Hors 5D 30
Dell, The RH6: Horl 3G 5
RH19: E Grin 4H 25
Dell La. RH14: Bill 3G 37
Delrogue Rd. RH11: Ifield 2D 14
Delta Bungs. RH6: Horl 6F 5
(off Delta Dr.)
Delta Dr. RH6: Horl 6F 5
Delta Ho. RH6: Horl 6F 5
(off Delta Dr.)
Dempsey Wlk. RH11: Craw 3D 14
Denchers Plat RH11: Craw 2G 15
Dene, The RH13: Southw 3C 36
Dene Cl. RH6: Horl 2D 4
Dene Tye RH10: Craw 4E 17
Denmans RH10: Craw 4E 17
Denne Pde. RH12: Hors 2G 33
DENNE PARK 2G 33
Denne Rd. RH11: Craw 6G 15
RH12: Hors 2G 33
Den Vale Trad. Pk. RH10: Craw 6H 15
Departures RH6: Gatw 1A 10
Depot Rd. RH11: Craw 2G 15
RH13: Hors 1A 34
Derwent Cl. RH11: Craw 6C 14
RH12: Hors 3D 30
Detling Rd. RH11: Craw 4F 21
Devonshire Rd. RH13: Hors 1II 33
Dewar Cl. RH11: Ifield 6B 14
Dew Pond Cl. RH13: Hors 6B 30
Dexter Dr. RH19: E Grin 5E 25
Diana Wlk. RH6: Horl 4G 5
(off High St.)
Dickens Rd. RH19: E Grin 4C 24
Dickens Rd. RH10: Craw 2G 21
Dickins Way RH13: Hors 3B 34
Dingle, The RH11: Craw 5E 15
Dingle Cl. RH11: Craw 4E 15
Dione Wlk. RH11: Craw 2B 20
Dirty La. RH19: Ash W 1E 27
Discovery Pk. RH10: Craw 6B 10
Ditchling Hill RH11: Craw 2F 21
Dobbins Pl. RH11: Ifield 6A 14

Dobson Rd. RH11: Craw 2G 15
Dolby Ter. RH6: Charlw 3B 8
Dollis Cl. RH10: Craw 6D 16
DOMEWOOD 4F 13
Doncaster Wlk. RH10: Craw 1B 22
Donkey La. RH6: Horl 2E 11
Donne Cl. RH10: Craw 3C 16
Donnington Ct. RH11: Craw 2C 20
Doomsday Gdn. RH13: Hors 2C 34
DOOMSDAY GREEN 3C 34
Doomsday La. RH13: Hors 3C 34
Dorking Rd. RH12: Warnh 1E 29
Dormans RH11: Craw 6D 14
Dormans Pk. Rd. RH19: E Grin 2D 24
Dorset Av. RH19: E Grin 2C 24
Dorset Gdns. RH19: E Grin 2C 24
Dorset M. RH19: E Grin 2C 24
Dorsten Pl. RH11: Craw 2B 20
Dorsten Sq. RH11: Craw 2C 20
Dove Cl. RH11: Craw 3G 15
Dovedale Cres. RH11: Craw 1E 21
Dover Cl. RH13: Southw 3B 36
Dower Wlk. RH11: Craw 6D 14
Dowlands La. RH6: Smallf 4G 7
RH10: Copt .4G 7
Downe Cl. RH6: Horl 2D 4
Downland Ct. RH11: Craw 1F 21
Downland Dr. RH11: Craw 1F 21
Downland Pl. RH11: Craw 1F 21
DOWN PARK 2F 19
Downs Link . . . . .6A 32 & 3A 36
Downsman Ct. RH10: Craw 2G 21
Downsview Cotts. RH14: Bill 3F 37
Downsview Rd. RH12: Hors 3D 30
Dragons Health Club
Copthorne 1H 17
Drake Cl. RH12: Hors 3A 30
Drake Rd. RH6: Horl 4D 4
RH10: Craw 1H 21
Driftway, The RH11: Craw 4G 15
Drive, The RH6: Horl 3G 5
RH10: Copt .6B 12
RH10: Craw .1B 16
Drummond Rd. RH11: Craw 6B 14
Drury Cl. RH10: Craw 1E 23
Duke Cl. RH10: Craw 3D 22
Dukes Head RH10: Craw D 6D 12
Dukes Sq. RH11: Craw 2G 33
Dulcima Ho. RH12: Hors 1G 33
Duncton Cl. RH11: Craw 3E 15
Dunnings Health & Fitness Club 6E 25
Dunning's Rd. RH19: E Grin 6E 25
Dunsfold Cl. RH11: Craw 6D 14
Durfold Rd. RH12: Hors 2H 29
Durham Cl. RH10: Craw 3H 21
(not continuous)
Durkins Rd. RH19: E Grin 2D 24
Dutchells Copse RH12: Hors 3A 30
Duxhurst La. RH2: Sid 1A 4
Dyers Almhouses RH10: Craw 4G 15
Dyers Fld. RH6: Smallf 4E 7
Dyson Wlk. RH11: Craw 4E 21

E

Eady Cl. RH13: Hors 1B 34
Eagle Est. RH14: Bill 4G 37
(off Brooker's Rd.)
Earle Ho. RH19: E Grin 3F 25
(off Badger's Way)
Earles Mdw. RH12: Hors 3C 30
Earlswood Cl. RH13: Hors 5B 30
Early Commons RH10: Craw 4A 16
(not continuous)
Eastbourne Rd. RH19: Felb 1A 24
East Court 3F 25
Eastcroft M. RH12: Hors 2D 32
Easteds La. RH13: Southw 3C 36
Eastgate M. RH13: Hors 2H 33
EAST GRINSTEAD 4E 25
East Grinstead Mus. 4F 25
East Grinstead Station (Rail) 4D 24
East Grinstead Town Mus. 3F 25
East Gun Copse RH13: Hors 6C 32
East Hill La. RH10: Copt 3C 12
East M. RH12: Hors 1G 33

Easton Cres. RH14: Bill 3H 37
East Pk. RH10: Craw 6G 15
East Pk. La. RH7: Newchap 1H 13
East St. RH10: Turn H 6H 19
RH12: Hors 2G 33
RH14: Bill .3G 37
Eastway RH6: Gatw 2C 10
Eastwood RH10: Craw 5A 16
Eddington Hill RH11: Craw 4D 20
Eden Rd. RH11: Craw 1C 20
Eden Va. RH19: E Grin 2D 24
(not continuous)
Edgar Cl. RH10: Worth 6F 17
Edinburgh Cl. RH13: Southw 4C 36
Edinburgh Ho. RH11: Craw 3E 21
Edinburgh Way RH19: E Grin 6F 25
Edrich Rd. RH11: Craw 4D 20
Effingham La. RH10: Copt 4D 12
Effingham Park Golf Course 5E 13
Effingham Rd. RH6: Copt 3B 12
RH10: Copt 3B 12
Elbourne Ho. RH6: Horl 4G 5
(off Lumley Rd.)
Elgar Way RH13: Hors 5D 30
Elger Way RH10: Copt 5H 11
Elgin Cl. RH13: Hors 6B 30
Elizabethan Way RH10: Craw 6D 16
Elizabeth Ct. RH6: Horl 4F 5
Elizabeth Cres. RH19: E Grin 2F 25
Elliot Cl. RH10: Craw 6D 16
Ellman Rd. RH11: Craw 1C 20
Ellson Cl. RH10: Craw 1D 22
Ellwood Pl. RH11: Craw 5C 14
Elm Ct. RH19: E Grin 3D 24
(Newlands Cres.)
RH19: E Grin 5E 25
(The Jordans)
Elmcroft Ct. RH10: Craw 5H 15
Elm Dr. RH19: E Grin 4G 25
Elm Gro. RH13: Hors 2A 34
Elm Tree Cl. RH6: Horl 3F 5
Elsted Cl. RH11: Craw 3E 15
Ely Cl. RH10: Craw 3H 21
Emberwood RH11: Craw 3F 15
Emlyn Rd. RH6: Horl 3D 4
Emsworth Cl. RH10: Craw 2D 22
Ends Pl. RH12: Warnh 1A 28
Enfield Rd. RH11: Craw 3E 21
Engalee RH19: E Grin 3C 24
Englefield RH12: Hors 1D 32
Ennerdale Cl. RH11: Craw 1E 21
Enterprise Centre, The RH10: Craw 1A 16
Enterprise Ct. RH11: Craw 1G 15
Enterprise Ho. RH12: Hors 2F 33
Epping Wlk. RH10: Craw 1A 22
Epsom Rd. RH10: Craw 1B 22
Erica Way RH10: Copt 6H 11
RH12: Hors 4H 29
Eridge Cl. RH10: Craw 5D 16
Ermenild Ho. RH19: E Grin 3E 25
Erskine Cl. RH11: Craw 3B 20
Eskdale Way RH10: Craw 1E 23
Estcots Dr. RH19: E Grin 4F 25
Evans Cl. RH10: Craw 6E 17
Evelyn Cl. RH19: Felb 6A 24
Evelyn Lancaster Ho. RH12: Hors 3A 30
Evelyn Wlk. RH10: Craw 2H 21
Eversfield RH13: Southw 4C 36
Eversfield Rd. RH13: Hors 2A 34
Ewelands RH6: Horl 3H 5
Ewhurst Cl. RH11: Craw 5F 15
Ewhurst Rd. RH11: Craw 5E 15
Excalibur Cl. RH11: Ifield 6B 14
Exchange Rd. RH11: Craw 5H 15
Exeter Cl. RH10: Craw 3H 21
Eyles Cl. RH12: Hors 5F 29

F

Fairbank Rd. RH13: Southw 4B 36
Fairfield Av. RH6: Horl 5F 5
Fairfield Rd. RH19: E Grin 5F 25
Fairlawn Cres. RH19: E Grin 3B 24
Fairlawn Dr. RH19: E Grin 3B 24
Fairlawns RH6: Horl 5G 5
Fairstone Ct. RH6: Horl 3G 5

Fair Vw. RH12: Hors 6E 29
Fairview Cotts. RH13: Southw 2D 36
Fairview Ct. RH19: E Grin 5F 25
   (off Fairfield Rd.)
Fairway RH10: Copt 1A 18
  RH11: Ifield 1A 20
Fairway Cl. RH10: Copt 1H 17
Falcon Cl. RH11: Craw 3G 15
Falklands Dr. RH13: Hors 5D 30
Fallow Deer Cl. RH13: Hors 6D 30
Fallowfield Way RH6: Horl 3G 5
Falmer Cl. RH11: Craw 1G 21
Falmouth M. RH13: Southw 4C 36
Famet Ct. RH19: E Grin 2C 24
Faraday Av. RH19: E Grin 6F 25
Faraday Cen., The RH10: Craw 2A 16
Faraday Ct. RH10: Craw 1H 15
Faraday Rd. RH10: Craw 1A 16
Farebrothers RH12: Warnh 1D 28
Farhalls Cres. RH12: Hors 4B 30
Farm Av. RH12: Hors 6F 29
Farm Cl. RH10: Craw 4B 16
  RH12: Warnh 2D 28
  RH19: E Grin 5H 25
Farmfield Cotts. RH6: Charlw 2E 9
Farmfield Dr. RH6: Charlw 1E 9
Farmleigh Cl. RH10: Craw 3D 16
Farm Wlk. RH6: Horl 4E 5
Farnham Cl. RH11: Craw 5F 21
Farriers Cl. RH14: Bill 4F 37
Farriers Ct. RH12: Hors 1G 33
Farthings Hill RH12: Hors 6D 28
   (off Guildford Rd.)
Farthings Hill Interchange
  RH12: Broadb H, Hors 6C 28
Farthings Wlk. RH12: Hors 6D 28
Faulkner Cl. RH11: Craw 5E 21
FAYGATE 1H 31
Fay Rd. RH12: Hors 4G 29
FELBRIDGE 1A 24
Felbridge Av. RH10: Craw 4E 17
Felbridge Cen., The RH19: E Grin 2A 24
Felbridge Cl. RH19: E Grin 2C 24
Felbridge Ct. RH19: E Grin 1A 24
Felcot Rd. RH19: Felb 6H 13
Feld, The RH19: E Grin 2A 24
Fellcott Way RH12: Hors 2D 32
Felwater Ct. RH19: E Grin 2A 24
Fenby Cl. RH13: Hors 5D 30
Fenchurch Rd. RH10: Craw 1C 22
Fender Ho. RH12: Hors 1F 33
Fenhurst Cl. RH12: Hors 2D 32
Fennel Cres. RH11: Craw 3E 21
Fermandy La. RH10: Craw D 2F 19
Ferndown RH6: Horl 2F 5
  RH10: Craw 1E 17
FERNHILL 2F 11
Fernhill Cl. RH10: Craw D 2G 19
Fernhill Rd. RH6: Horl 2E 11
Fernhurst Cl. RH11: Craw 3E 15
Fern Way RH12: Hors 4H 29
Feroners Cl. RH10: Craw 1B 22
Feroners Ct. RH10: Craw 1B 22
   (off Feroners Cl.)
Ferring Cl. RH11: Craw 4E 15
Festival Cl. RH10: Craw 1D 22
Field Bank RH6: Horl 2G 5
Field Cl. RH6: Horl 2H 5
Fieldend RH12: Hors 4C 30
Fieldings, The RH6: Horl 3G 5
  RH13: Southw 6B 36
FIELD PLACE .4B 28
Field Pl. Cotts. RH12: Broadb H 4B 28
Fieldview RH6: Horl 3G 5
Field Wlk. RH6: Horl 4E 5
   (off Court Lodge Rd.)
  RH6: Smallf .3F 7
Filbert Cres. RH11: Craw 5D 14
Filey Cl. RH11: Craw 1C 20
Finch Cres. RH10: Turn H 6H 19
Findon Cl. RH11: Craw 3E 15
Findon Way RH12: Broadb H 6B 28
Finlat Cl. RH10: Craw 5A 16
Finsbury Cl. RH11: Craw 3F 21
Firbank Way RH19: E Grin 4D 24
Firlands RH6: Horl 3G 5
Firle Cl. RH10: Craw 3H 15

Fir Tree Cl. RH11: Craw 2E 15
Fisher Cl. RH10: Craw 1H 21
Fishers Ct. RH12: Hors 5G 29
Fitchet Cl. RH11: Craw 3E 15
Fitzalan Pl. RH10: Worth 5E 17
Fitzalan Rd. RH13: Hors 5C 30
Five Acres RH12: Hors 3H 15
Five Oaks Rd.
  RH13: Slinf, Itch, Broadb H 1A 32
Flamsteed Hgts. RH11: Craw 4D 20
Fleming Centre, The RH10: Craw 1H 15
Fleming Wlk. RH19: E Grin 6F 25
Fleming Way RH10: Craw 1H 15
Fleming Way Ind. Cen. RH10: Craw 6A 10
Fleming Way Rdbt. RH10: Craw 1G 15
Fletcher Cl. RH10: Craw 1H 21
Fletcher Rd. RH13: Southw 4B 36
   (off College Rd.)
Fletchers RH13: Southw 2B 36
Fletchers Cl. RH13: Hors 2A 34
Flint Cl. RH6: Horl 2H 5
  RH10: Craw 2C 22
Fontana Cl. RH10: Worth 6E 17
Fontwell Rd. RH10: Craw 2B 22
Forbes Cl. RH10: Craw 3C 22
Fordingbridge Cl. RH12: Hors 2G 33
Forest Cl. RH10: Craw D 3G 19
  RH12: Hors 5D 30
  RH13: Mann H 5E 35
Forester Rd. RH10: Craw 1H 21
Foresters, The RH13: Hors 2B 34
Forestfield RH10: Craw 2C 22
  RH13: Hors 6C 30
Forest Grange RH13: Hors, Colg 4F 31
Forest Grange Mnr. RH13: Colg 5G 31
Forest Lodge RH19: E Grin 5F 25
Forest M. RH12: Hors 4D 30
Forest Oaks RH13: Hors 5D 30
Forest Pk. RH13: Mann H 5G 35
Forest Recreational Cen. 2B 34
Forest Rd. RH11: Pease P 6A 20
  RH12: Hors, Colg 5D 30
  RH12: Pease P 6A 20
  RH18: F Row 6H 27
FOREST ROW .4F 27
Forest Row Bus. Pk. RH18: F Row 4F 27
Forest Vw. RH10: Craw 2B 22
Forest Vw. Rd. RH19: E Grin 6E 25
Forest Way RH18: F Row 3C 26
  RH19: E Grin 6G 25
Forge, The RH6: Charlw 2B 8
  RH12: Warnh 1C 28
  RH13: Southw 4B 36
Forge Cl. RH12: Broadb H 5B 28
Forge Cotts. RH12: Broadb H 5B 28
   (off Forge Cl.)
Forge La. RH10: Craw 4B 16
  RH12: Broadb H 5B 28
Forge Pl. RH6: Hookw 6D 4
Forge Rd. RH10: Craw 4B 16
Forge Way RH14: Bill 3F 37
Forge Wood RH10: Craw 6E 11
Forge Wood Ind. Est. RH10: Craw 1C 16
Forum, The RH12: Hors 1G 33
Fosters Pl. E. RH19: E Grin 3D 24
Foundry Cl. RH13: Hors 5A 30
Foundry Ct. RH13: Hors 6A 30
Foundry La. RH13: Hors 6A 30
Fountains Cl. RH11: Craw 1D 20
Four Oaks RH18: F Row 5F 27
Fowler Cl. RH10: Craw 1D 22
Fox Cl. RH11: Craw 2E 15
Foxes Cl. RH13: Southw 6B 36
Foxfield Cotts. RH13: Southw 6B 36
Foxglove Av. RH12: Hors 3A 30
Foxglove Wlk. RH11: Craw 2E 21
Foxleigh Chase RH12: Hors 5B 30
Framfield Cl. RH11: Craw 3D 14
Francis Edwards Way RH11: Craw 3B 20
Franklin Rd. RH10: Craw 6D 16
Freeman Rd. RH12: Warnh 1D 28
Frenches M. RH14: Bill 3F 37
Frenches Mead RH14: Bill 3F 37
Frenches Rdbt. RH14: Bill 3F 37
Freshfield Bank RH18: F Row 5E 27
Freshfield Cl. RH10: Craw 6B 16

Freshlands RH14: Bill 3F 37
Freshwater Pde. RH12: Hors 1F 33
   (off Bishopric)
Friars Rookery RH10: Craw 5A 16
Friary Way RH10: Craw 6G 15
Friday St. RH12: Warnh 2C 28
Friends Cl. RH11: Craw 2G 15
Friston Wlk. RH11: Craw 3D 14
Frith Pk. RH19: E Grin 2E 25
Fry Cl. RH11: Craw 4E 21
Fryern Rd. RH19: Felb 6G 13
Fuel Farm Rd. RH6: Gatw 6D 4
Fulham Cl. RH11: Craw 3E 21
Fulmar Cl. RH11: Ifield 6A 14
Fulmar Dr. RH19: E Grin 2G 25
Furlong Way RH6: Gatw 1A 10
Furnace Dr. RH10: Craw 1A 22
Furnace Farm Rd. RH10: Craw 1B 22
FURNACE GREEN 1B 22
Furnace Pde. RH10: Craw 1B 22
Furnace Pl. RH10: Craw 1B 22
FURNACE WOOD 5H 13
Furze Cl. RH6: Horl 4A 6
Furzefield RH11: Craw 4E 15
Furzefield Rd. RH12: Hors 4D 30
  RH19: E Grin 1D 24
Furze La. RH19: E Grin 1B 24

G

Gables, The RH6: Horl 5F 5
  RH10: Copt 6A 12
  RH12: Hors 5H 29
  RH13: Southw 5B 36
Gabriel Rd. RH10: Craw 3D 22
Gage Cl. RH10: Craw D 2H 19
Gage Ridge RH18: F Row 5E 27
Gaggle Wood RH13: Mann H 5E 35
Gainsborough Rd. RH10: Craw 3A 22
Galahad Rd. RH11: Ifield 5B 14
Gales Dr. RH10: Craw 5A 16
Gales Pl. RH10: Craw 5A 16
Ganymede Ct. RH11: Craw 2B 20
Garden Cl. RH19: E Grin 6F 25
Gardener Ho. RH13: Southw 4A 36
   (off College Rd.)
Gardeners Cl. RH12: Warnh 1C 28
Gardeners Ct. RH13: Hors 2H 33
Garden Ho. La. RH19: E Grin 6F 25
Garden Pl. RH12: Hors 5G 29
Garden Wlk. RH11: Craw 5F 15
  RH12: Hors 5G 29
Garden Wood Rd. RH19: E Grin 4B 24
Gardner La. RH10: Craw D 3F 19
Garland Ct. RH19: E Grin 4D 24
   (off Garland Rd.)
Garland Rd. RH19: E Grin 3D 24
Garrett Cl. RH10: Craw 1D 22
Garrick Wlk. RH10: Craw 2H 21
Garrones, The RH10: Craw 4E 17
Garton Cl. RH11: Ifield 6B 14
Gasson Wood Rd. RH11: Craw 1B 20
Gateford Dr. RH12: Hors 3B 30
Gates Cl. RH10: Craw 3D 22
GATWICK AIRPORT
  North Terminal 1H 9
  South Terminal 2B 10
Gatwick Airport Beehive Area
  RH6: Craw 4B 10
Gatwick Airport Station (Rail) 2C 10
Gatwick Aviation Mus. 3C 8
Gatwick Bus. Pk. RH6: Craw 5C 10
  RH6: Hookw 5B 4
Gatwick Ga. RH11: Low H 4H 9
Gatwick Ga. Ind. Est. RH11: Low H 4H 9
   (not continuous)
Gatwick Intl. Distribution Cen.
  RH10: Craw 5C 10
Gatwick Metro Cen. RH6: Horl 4G 5
GATWICK PARK SPIRE HOSPITAL 5D 4
Gatwick Rd. RH6: Craw 4B 10
  RH10: Craw 6B 10
Gatwick Rd. Rdbt. RH6: Craw 4B 10
Gatwick Way RH6: Gatw 1A 10
Geary Cl. RH6: Smallf 6E 7
Gemini Cl. RH11: Craw 1B 20

Genesis Bus. Cen. RH13: Hors 6B 30
George Pinion Ct. RH12: Hors 6F 29
Georgian Cl. RH10: Craw 6E 17
Gerald Ct. RH13: Hors 1A 34
Ghyll Ct. *RH13: Southw* *4B 36*
            (off Station Rd.)
Ghyll Cres. RH13: Hors 3B 34
Gibbons Cl. RH10: Craw 2D 22
Giblets La. RH12: Hors 2B 30
Giblets Way RH12: Hors 2A 30
Gibson Pl. RH10: Craw 3H 15
Giffards Cl. RH19: E Grin 4F 25
Gilham La. RH18: F Row 5E 27
Gillett Ct. RH13: Hors 5D 30
Gilligan Cl. RH10: Craw 1F 33
Gillmans Ind. Est. RH14: Bill 5G 37
Ginhams Rd. RH11: Craw 5E 15
Glade, The RH10: Craw 1B 22
    RH13: Hors 6C 30
Glades, The RH19: E Grin 4H 25
Gladstone Rd. RH12: Hors 6H 29
Glanville Wlk. RH11: Craw 2D 20
Gleave Cl. RH19: E Grin 3G 25
Glebe, The RH6: Horl 4E 5
    RH10: Copt 6A 12
    RH19: Felb 1A 24
Glebe Cl. RH10: Craw 4H 15
Glebelands RH10: Craw D 4F 19
Glen, The RH13: Southw 3C 36
Glendale Cl. RH12: Hors 3C 30
Glendon Ho. RH10: Craw 6G 15
Glendyne Cl. RH19: E Grin 5G 25
Glendyne Way RH19: E Grin 5G 25
Gleneagles Ct. RH10: Craw 6G 15
Glenfield Cotts. RH6: Charlw 2A 8
Glenview Ct. RH10: Craw 3A 16
Glen Vue RH19: E Grin 4E 25
Gloucester Cl. RH19: E Grin 5G 25
Gloucester Rd. RH10: Craw 3H 21
Glover's Rd. RH6: Charlw 2A 8
Glynde Ho. RH10: Craw 3H 15
Glynde Pl. *RH12: Hors* *1G 33*
            (off South St.)
Goddard Cl. RH10: Craw 2C 22
Godolphin Ct. RH10: Craw 1G 21
Godwin Way RH13: Hors 5B 30
Goepel Ct. RH10: Craw 4B 16
Goffs Cl. RH11: Craw 6F 15
Goffs La. RH11: Craw 5E 15
         (not continuous)
Goffs Park 6E 15
Goffs Pk. Rd. RH11: Craw 6F 15
Goldcrest Cl. RH6: Horl 3D 4
Goldfinch Cl. RH10: Craw 3G 15
    RH12: Hors 2G 29
Golding Cl. RH10: Craw 6D 16
Golding La. RH13: Mann H 5E 35
Golding's Hill RH13: Mann H 4F 35
Gonville Works RH6: Smallf 5E 7
Goodwin Cl. RH11: Craw 2C 20
Goodwins Cl. RH19: E Grin 2D 24
Goodwood Cl. RH10: Craw 2B 22
GOOSE GREEN 3C 28
Goosegreen Cl. RH12: Hors 4H 29
Gordon Rd. RH12: Hors 5H 29
Goring's Mead RH13: Hors 2H 33
Gorling Cl. RH11: Ifield 6B 14
Gorringes Brook RH12: Hors 3H 29
Gorse Cl. RH10: Copt 1A 18
    RH11: Craw 5E 21
Gorse Dr. RH6: Smallf 4E 7
Gorse End RH12: Hors 4H 29
Gorselands RH14: Bill 3H 37
Gosden Cl. RH10: Craw 6B 16
Gossops Dr. RH11: Craw 6C 14
GOSSOPS GREEN 6C 14
Gossops Grn. La. RH11: Craw 6D 14
Gossops Pde. *RH11: Craw* *6C 14*
         (off Gossops Dr.)
Goudhurst Cl. RH10: Worth 5F 17
Goudhurst Keep RH10: Worth 5F 17
Gower Rd. RH6: Horl 4D 4
Grace Ct. RH12: Hors 5C 30
Grace Rd. RH11: Craw 4D 20
Graffham Cl. RH11: Craw 3E 15
Granary Cl. RH6: Horl 2F 5
    RH12: Hors 2D 32

Granary Way RH12: Hors 2D 32
Grand Pde. RH10: Craw 5G 15
Grange, The RH6: Horl 1G 5
Grange Cl. RH10: Craw 3B 16
Grange Cres. RH10: Craw D 4G 19
Grange End RH6: Smallf 4D 6
Grange Rd. RH10: Craw D 4F 19
Grange Way RH6: Smallf 4D 6
    RH13: Southw 3B 36
Grasmere Ct. *RH10: Craw* *1E 23*
          (off Grayrigg Rd.)
Grasmere Gdns. RH12: Hors 3D 30
Grasslands RH6: Smallf 4D 6
Grassmere RH6: Horl 3H 5
Grattons Dr. RH10: Craw 2D 16
Gratwicke Cl. RH14: Bill 3G 37
Graveney Rd. RH10: Craw 6D 16
Gravetye Cl. RH10: Craw 1B 22
Grayrigg Rd. RH10: Craw 1E 23
Grays Wood RH6: Horl 4H 5
Gt. Daux Rdbt. RH12: Warnh 2F 29
Great Fld. Pl. RH19: E Grin 2H 25
Great Grooms RH14: Bill 5F 37
Greatham Rd. RH10: Craw 2D 22
Great Ho. Ct. RH6: Horl 5F 25
Greatlake Ct. *RH6: Horl* *3G 5*
         (off Tanyard Way)
Gt. Lime Kilns RH13: Southw 4C 36
Grebe Cres. RH13: Hors 2C 34
Grecians E. *RH13: Hors* *6C 32*
       (off East Gun Copse)
Grecians W. *RH13: Hors* *6B 32*
      (off West Gun Copse)
Green, The RH10: Copt 6A 12
    RH11: Craw 4F 15
Greenacres RH10: Craw 5G 29
    RH12: Hors 5G 29
Green Cl. RH13: Southw 2B 36
Greenfields Cl. RH6: Horl 2D 4
    RH12: Hors 3C 30
Greenfields Rd. RH6: Horl 2E 5
Greenfields Way RH12: Hors 3C 30
Greenfinch Way RH12: Hors 2G 29
Green Hedges Av. RH19: E Grin 3D 24
Green Hedges Cl. RH19: E Grin 3D 24
Green La. RH6: Ship B 2G 11
    RH10: Craw 3H 15
    RH10: Craw D 5E 13
    RH10: Worth 5E 17
         (not continuous)
    RH13: Southw 6E 33
Greens La. RH13: Mann H 4F 35
Greenstede Av. RH19: E Grin 2F 25
Green Vw., The RH11: Pease P 6F 21
Green Wlk. RH10: Craw 3H 15
Greenway RH12: Hors 6F 29
Greenways Wlk. RH11: Craw 4F 21
Greenwich Cl. RH11: Craw 3F 21
Greenwood Ct. RH11: Craw 4E 21
Gregory Cl. RH10: Craw 3D 22
Gregsons RH12: Warnh 1C 28
Grendon Cl. RH6: Horl 2E 5
Gresham Wlk. RH10: Craw 2H 21
         (not continuous)
Greyhound Slip RH10: Craw 4E 17
Grier Cl. RH11: Ifield 6B 14
Griffiths Path RH18: F Row 5E 27
Grisedale Ct. RH11: Craw 1F 21
Groombridge Way RH12: Hors 2D 32
Grooms, The RH12: Hors 3E 17
Groomsland Dr. RH14: Bill 5F 37
Grosvenor Cl. RH6: Horl 6F 5
Grosvenor Ct. *RH19: E Grin* *4D 24*
        (off Grosvenor Rd.)
Grosvenor Rd. RH19: E Grin 4D 24
Grouse Rd. RH13: Plum P, Colg 4H 35
Grove, The RH6: Horl 5G 5
    RH11: Craw 5F 15
Grove Ct. RH10: Craw 5B 16
Grovelands RH6: Horl 5G 5
Grove Rd. RH6: Horl 3D 4
Guernsey Cl. RH11: Craw 3D 20
Guildford Ct. RH12: Hors 6D 28
    RH12: Slinf, Broadb H 4A 28
Guillemot Path RH11: Ifield 6A 14
Guinevere Rd. RH11: Ifield 5B 14

Guinness Ct. RH11: Craw 3F 21
Gunning Cl. RH11: Craw 2D 20
Gwynne Gdns. RH19: E Grin 3C 24

H

Hackenden Cl. RH19: E Grin 2E 25
Hackenden Cotts. RH19: E Grin 2E 25
Hackenden La. RH19: E Grin 3E 25
         (not continuous)
Hadmans Cl. RH12: Hors 2G 33
Halfacres RH10: Craw 4H 15
Halifax Cl. RH10: Craw 2F 17
Halland Cl. RH10: Craw 4B 16
Halley Cl. RH11: Craw 4E 21
Hallsland RH10: Craw D 3H 19
Halnaker Wlk. RH11: Craw 2C 20
Halsford Cft. RH19: E Grin 2B 24
Halsford Grn. RH19: E Grin 2B 24
Halsford La. RH19: E Grin 3B 24
Halsford Pk. Rd. RH19: E Grin 3C 24
Hambleton Cl. RH11: Craw 1F 21
Hambleton Hill RH11: Craw 1F 21
Hamilton Cl. RH6: Horl 5F 5
Hamilton Rd. RH12: Hors 6F 29
Hammerpond Rd.
    RH13: Hors, Colg, Mann H 2B 34
    RH13: Plum P 4H 35
Hammerwood Rd. RH19: Ash W 1D 26
Hammer Yd. RH10: Craw 6G 15
Hammond Rd. RH11: Craw 5E 21
Hampden Cl. RH10: Craw 2F 17
Hampers Ct. RH13: Hors 1H 33
Hamper's La. RH13: Hors 1C 34
Hampstead Wlk. RH11: Craw 3F 21
Hampton Lodge RH6: Horl 5F 5
Hampton Way RH19: E Grin 6F 25
Hanbury Rd. RH11: Ifield 6B 14
Hanover Cl. RH10: Craw 1A 22
         (not continuous)
Hanover Ct. RH13: Hors 6B 30
Hansworth Ho. *RH10: Craw* *6B 16*
        (off Brighton Rd.)
Hardham Cl. RH11: Craw 3D 14
Hard's Hill RH10: Hors 6H 33
Hardy Cl. RH6: Horl 4D 4
    RH10: Craw 4D 16
    RH12: Hors 5F 29
Hare La. RH11: Craw 2E 15
Harewood Cl. RH10: Craw 2B 16
Harmans Dr. RH19: E Grin 4H 25
Harmans Mead RH19: E Grin 4H 25
Harmony Cl. RH11: Craw 1B 20
Harold Rd. RH10: Worth 6F 17
Haroldslea RH6: Horl 6A 6
Haroldslea Cl. RH6: Horl 6H 5
Haroldslea Dr. RH6: Horl 6H 5
Harper Dr. RH10: Craw 3D 22
Harrier Ct. *RH10: Craw* *2E 17*
        (off Bristol Cl.)
Harris Cl. RH11: Craw 2E 21
Harris Path RH11: Craw 2E 21
Harrowsley Ct. RH6: Horl 3G 5
Harrowsley Grn. La. RH6: Horl 5H 5
Hartfield Rd. RH18: F Row 4F 27
Harting Cl. RH11: Craw 2C 20
Harvesters RH12: Hors 5H 29
Harvest Hill RH19: E Grin 5E 25
Harvest Rd. RH10: Craw 1D 22
Harvestside RH6: Horl 3H 5
Harvey Cl. RH11: Craw 4D 20
Harwood Rd. RH13: Hors 6A 30
Harwoods Cl. RH19: E Grin 6F 25
Harwoods La. RH19: E Grin 6F 25
Hascombe Ct. RH11: Craw 6D 14
Haslett Av. E. RH10: Craw 5H 15
Haslett Av. W. RH10: Craw 6G 15
Hassocks Ct. RH11: Craw 2C 20
Hastings Rd. RH10: Craw 5D 16
Hatch End RH18: F Row 5F 27
Hatchgate RH6: Horl 5E 5
Hatchlands RH12: Hors 2C 30
Hatfield Wlk. RH11: Craw 2B 20
Hathersham Cl. RH6: Smallf 3D 6
Hathersham La. RH6: Smallf 1A 6
Haven Gdns. RH10: Craw D 2G 19

Havengate RH12: Hors ...4B 30
Haversham Cl. RH10: Craw ...5A 16
Haversham Ho. RH6: Horl ...2G 5
Hawarden Cl. RH10: Craw D ...3H 19
Haweswater Pl. RH10: Craw ...1E 23
(off Castlerigg Way)
Hawkesbourne Rd. RH12: Hors ...4B 30
Hawkesmoor Rd. RH11: Craw ...1B 20
Hawkhurst Wlk. RH10: Craw ...1C 22
Hawkins Rd. RH10: Craw ...2H 21
Hawmead RH10: Craw D ...3H 19
Haworth Rd. RH10: Craw ...6C 16
Hawth Av. RH10: Craw ...1H 21
Hawth Cl. RH10: Craw ...1H 21
Hawthorn Cl. RH11: Craw ...2F 15
　RH12: Hors ...5G 29
Hawth Theatre ...6A 16
Haybarn Dr. RH12: Hors ...2A 30
Hayes Wlk. RH6: Smallf ...3D 6
Hayfields RH6: Horl ...3G 5
Hayling Ct. RH11: Craw ...2F 21
Haywards RH10: Craw ...2E 17
Hazel Cl. RH10: Craw D ...3H 19
　RH11: Craw ...2F 15
　RH13: Southw ...4C 36
Hazelhurst RH6: Horl ...3H 5
Hazelhurst Cres. RH12: Hors ...2D 32
Hazelhurst Dr. RH6: Worth ...5F 17
Hazel Way RH10: Craw D ...3H 19
Hazelwick Av. RH10: Craw ...3B 16
Hazelwick Ct. RH10: Craw ...3B 16
(off Hazelwick Av.)
Hazelwick M. RH10: Craw ...3B 16
Hazelwick Mill La. RH10: Craw ...3B 16
(not continuous)
Hazelwick Rd. RH10: Craw ...4B 16
Hazelwick Rdbt. RH10: Craw ...3B 16
Hazelwood RH11: Craw ...5D 14
Hazelwood Cl. RH10: Craw D ...3E 19
Headley Cl. RH10: Craw ...2E 17
Heath Cl. RH12: Broadb H ...6C 28
　RH13: Mann H ...5F 35
Heathcote Dr. RH19: E Grin ...3B 24
Heathcotes RH10: Craw ...1E 23
Heath Ct. RH12: Broadb H ...6C 28
Heather Cl. RH10: Copt ...1A 18
　RH12: Hors ...4H 29
Heatherlands RH6: Horl ...3G 5
(not continuous)
Heatherleigh Ct. RH12: Hors ...5G 29
(off North Pde.)
Heather Wlk. RH6: Smallf ...4F 7
　RH11: Craw ...2E 21
Heathfield RH10: Craw ...2E 17
(not continuous)
Heath Way RH12: Hors ...4H 29
Hectors La. RH19: E Grin ...6H 25
Hedgecourt Pl. RH19: Felb ...6A 24
Hedgeside RH11: Craw ...4F 21
Hedingham Cl. RH6: Horl ...3H 5
Helicon Ho. RH11: Craw ...6F 15
Hemsby Wlk. RH10: Craw ...1C 22
Henbane Ct. RH11: Craw ...3D 20
Henderson Rd. RH11: Craw ...4E 21
Henderson Way RH12: Hors ...3D 32
Hengist Cl. RH12: Hors ...2E 33
Henley Cl. RH10: Craw ...2E 23
Henshaw Cl. RH11: Craw ...1C 20
Henson Rd. RH10: Craw ...4C 16
Henty Cl. RH11: Craw ...2B 20
Hepplewhite Cl. RH11: Craw ...4E 21
Hereford Cl. RH10: Craw ...3H 21
Heritage Lawn RH6: Horl ...3H 5
Herm Cl. RH11: Craw ...3D 20
Hermitage La. RH19: E Grin ...5F 25
Hermitage Rd. RH19: E Grin ...2D 24
Hermits Rd. RH10: Craw ...4A 16
Hernbrook Dr. RH13: Hors ...3A 34
Heron Cl. RH11: Craw ...3F 15
Heron Pl. RH19: E Grin ...5F 25
Herons Cl. RH10: Copt ...4F 13
Herons Lea RH10: Copt ...4F 13
Heronswood Ct. RH6: Horl ...3G 5
Herontye Dr. RH19: E Grin ...5F 25
Herontye Ho. RH19: E Grin ...6F 25
Heron Way RH13: Hors ...1C 34
Herrick Cl. RH10: Craw ...3D 16

Herschel Wlk. RH11: Craw ...4E 21
Hertford Ho. RH13: Hors ...5C 32
(off The Avenue)
Hevers Av. RH6: Horl ...3E 5
Hevers Cnr. RH6: Horl ...3E 5
Hewells Ct. RH12: Hors ...2G 33
Hexham Cl. RH10: Craw ...5F 17
Hickling Wlk. RH10: Craw ...1C 22
Higgins Way RH13: Hors ...2A 34
Highams Hill RH11: Craw ...6C 14
Highbirch Cl. RH12: Hors ...4D 30
Highdown Ct. RH10: Craw ...2C 22
Highdown Way RH12: Hors ...3B 30
Highfield Ho. RH11: Craw ...4G 15
(off Town Mead)
Highfield Rd. RH19: E Grin ...2D 24
Highfields RH18: F Row ...5F 27
Highgate Ct. RH11: Craw ...3F 21
Highgate Rd. RH18: F Row ...6E 27
Highgate Works RH18: F Row ...6E 27
HIGHGREEN ...6F 27
Highlands Av. RH13: Hors ...1A 34
Highlands Cres. RH13: Hors ...1A 34
Highlands Rd. RH13: Hors ...1A 34
High Oaks RH11: Craw ...1E 21
High Seat Copse RH14: Bill ...2G 37
High Seat Gdns. RH14: Bill ...2G 37
High St. RH6: Horl ...4G 5
　RH10: Craw ...5G 15
　RH14: Bill ...3G 37
　RH17: Bal ...6F 23
　RH19: E Grin ...5F 25
High Trees Ct. RH6: Sid ...3A 4
Highwood Pk. RH11: Craw ...3F 21
Highworth RH13: Hors ...2B 34
Hilda Duke's Way RH19: E Grin ...2E 25
Hilland Rdbt. RH14: Bill ...1G 37
Hillary Cl. RH19: E Grin ...2G 25
Hillcrest Cl. RH10: Craw ...5E 17
Hillfield Cotts. RH13: Itch ...3A 32
Hill Ho. Cl. RH10: Turn H ...6F 19
Hillingdale RH11: Craw ...4F 21
Hill Mead RH12: Hors ...6E 29
Hillmead RH11: Craw ...6C 14
Hill Pl. RH11: Craw ...6C 14
Hills Farm La. RH12: Hors ...2D 32
Hillside RH10: Craw D ...3G 19
　RH12: Hors ...1E 33
　RH18: F Row ...4F 27
Hillside Cl. RH11: Craw ...1E 21
　RH19: E Grin ...2E 25
Hills Pl. RH12: Hors ...1E 33
Hillview RH18: F Row ...6F 27
Hillview Gdns. RH11: Craw ...5F 21
Hilton Cl. RH6: Horl ...3H 5
Hindhead Cl. RH11: Craw ...1F 21
Hobbs Rd. RH11: Craw ...4D 20
Hocken Mead RH10: Craw ...3E 17
Hodgkin Cl. RH10: Craw ...6D 16
Hogarth Rd. RH10: Craw ...2A 22
Hog's Hill RH10: Craw ...2G 21
Hogshill Gdns. RH10: Craw ...1G 21
Holbein Rd. RH10: Craw ...2A 22
HOLBROOK ...1A 30
Holbrook Club, The ...3A 30
Holbrook School La.
　RH12: Hors ...2H 29
Holcroft Ct. RH19: E Grin ...1F 25
Holder Rd. RH10: Craw ...2C 22
Holders Ct. RH14: Bill ...2F 37
Hollands Ct. RH19: E Grin ...1G 25
Hollands Fld. RH12: Broadb H ...5C 28
Hollands Way RH12: Warnh ...1D 28
　RH19: E Grin ...1G 25
Hollie Cl. RH6: Smallf ...5E 7
Hollin Ct. RH10: Craw ...2H 15
Hollingbourne Cres. RH11: Craw ...5F 21
Hollow, The RH11: Craw ...6C 14
Hollybush Bus. Cen. RH10: Ship B ...5G 11
Hollybush Cl. RH10: Craw ...4H 15
Hollybush Rd. RH10: Craw ...4H 15
Holly Cl. RH10: Craw ...3B 16
　RH10: Craw ...4D 30
Hollywood Bowl
　Crawley ...4G 15
Holman Cl. RH11: Craw ...1F 21
Holmbury Cl. RH11: Craw ...1F 21

Holmbury Keep RH6: Horl ...3H 5
(off Maize Cft.)
Holmbush Cl. RH12: Hors ...3H 29
Holmbush Potteries Ind. Est.
　RH12: Fay ...4A 20
Holmcroft RH10: Craw ...6H 15
Holming End RH12: Hors ...4D 30
Holtye Av. RH19: E Grin ...2F 25
Holtye Pl. RH19: E Grin ...2G 25
Holtye Rd. RH19: E Grin ...3F 25
Holtye Wlk. RH10: Craw ...1B 22
Holyrood RH19: E Grin ...6G 25
Holyrood Pl. RH11: Craw ...3E 21
Home Cl. RH10: Craw ...3D 16
Home Farm Ho. RH12: Hors ...1G 33
(off Springfield Rd.)
Homefield Cl. RH6: Horl ...3G 5
Homestream Ho. RH12: Hors ...2F 33
Homethorne Ho. RH11: Craw ...6F 15
Honeysuckle Cl. RH6: Horl ...3H 5
Honeysuckle La. RH11: Craw ...2F 15
Honeysuckle Wlk. RH12: Hors ...4C 30
Honeywood Rd. RH13: Hors ...5C 30
HOOKWOOD ...5C 4
Hope Ct. RH11: Craw ...4E 21
Hophurst Cl. RH10: Craw D ...3G 19
Hophurst Dr. RH10: Craw D ...3G 19
Hophurst Hill RH10: Craw D ...1H 19
Hophurst La. RH10: Craw D ...3G 19
Hopkins Ct. RH11: Craw ...4E 21
Hop Oast (Horsham)
　(Park & Ride) ...5E 33
Hop Oast Rdbt. RH13: Hors ...6E 33
Hordern Ho. RH12: Hors ...2E 33
HORLEY ...4G 5
Horley Leisure Cen. ...4D 4
Horley Rd. RH6: Charlw ...3C 8
Horley Row RH6: Horl ...3E 5
Horley Station (Rail) ...5G 5
Hornbeam Cl. RH13: Hors ...2B 34
Hornbrook Copse RH13: Hors ...3B 34
Hornbrook Hill RH13: Hors ...3B 34
Horndean Cl. RH10: Craw ...1E 17
HORNE ...2H 7
Hornets, The RH13: Hors ...2H 33
Horse Hill RH6: Sid ...3A 4
Horseshoe Cl. RH10: Craw ...4E 17
HORSHAM ...1G 33
Horsham Gates RH13: Hors ...6A 30
Horsham Golf Course ...5F 33
HORSHAM HOSPITAL ...6G 29
Horsham Indoor Bowls Cen. ...1B 32
Horsham Mus. ...2G 33
(off Morth Gdns.)
Horsham Northern By-Pass
　RH12: Warnh, Hors ...3F 29
Horsham Rd. RH11: Craw ...3B 20
　RH11: Pease P ...6D 20
Horsham Station (Rail) ...6H 29
Horsham Trad. Est. RH13: Hors ...5A 30
Hoskins Pl. RH19: E Grin ...1G 25
Houghton Rd. RH10: Craw ...2D 22
Housman Way RH19: Felb ...6B 24
Howard Rd. RH11: Craw ...3B 20
　RH13: Hors ...5C 30
Howlands Ct. RH10: Craw ...5A 14
Hoylake Cl. RH11: Ifield ...6A 14
Hoyland Ho. RH11: Craw ...5C 1
Hudson Rd. RH11: Craw ...1H 2
Huffwood Trad. Est. RH14: Bill ...4G 3
Hunstanton Cl. RH11: Ifield ...6A 1
Hunter Ho. RH10: Craw ...2G 2
Hunter Rd. RH10: Craw ...2G 2
Hurst-An-Clays RH19: E Grin ...5E 2
Hurst Av. RH12: Hors ...6H 2
Hurst Cl. RH11: Craw ...1C 2
Hurst Ct. RH12: Hors ...6H 2
Hurst Farm Rd. RH19: E Grin ...5D 2
Hurstlands RH14: Bill ...4F 3
Hurst Pk. RH12: Hors ...6H 2
Hurst Rd. RH6: Horl ...3D
　RH12: Hors ...5G 2
Hutchins Way RH6: Horl ...2E
Huxley's (Bird of Prey & Garden) ...3B
Hyde Dr. RH11: Ifield ...6B
Hyde Heath Ct. RH11: Craw ...3E
Hylands Cl. RH10: Craw ...6B

Hyndman Cl. RH11: Craw 5E 21
Hyperion Ct. RH11: Craw 1B 20
Hyperion Wlk. RH6: Horl 6G 5

I

Icklesham Ho. RH11: Craw 2C 20
(off Salvington Rd.)
IFIELD 4D 14
Ifield Av. RH11: Craw 2D 14
Ifield Barn Theatre 3C 14
Ifield Dr. RH11: Craw, Ifield 4C 14
Ifield Golf Course 5B 14
IFIELD GREEN .3D 14
Ifield Grn. RH11: Craw, Ifield 2D 14
Ifield Pk. RH11: Craw 5C 14
Ifield Pond 6B 14
Ifield Rd. RH6: Charlw 5B 8
RH10: Craw 5G 15
RH11: Craw 4E 15
Ifield Rd. Rdbt. RH11: Craw 5G 15
Ifield Rdbt. RH11: Craw 4F 15
Ifield Station (Rail) 5D 14
Ifield St. RH11: Ifield 3C 14
Ifield Watermill 6B 14
IFIELDWOOD 2A 14
Ifield Wood RH11: Ifield 3A 14
Imberhorne Bus. Cen. RH19: E Grin 3B 24
Imberhorne La. RH19: E Grin 2B 24
Imberhorne Way RH19: E Grin 2B 24
Independent Bus. Pk., The
RH19: E Grin 3F 24
Infirmary Dr. RH13: Hors 5C 32
Ingram Cl. RH12: Hors 1E 33
Inholmes RH10: Craw 5B 16
Inkpen La. RH18: F Row 6F 27
Innes Rd. RH12: Hors 5B 30
Institute Wlk. RH19: E Grin 4E 25
International Dr. RH10: Craw 6H 15
Iona Cl. RH11: Craw 2E 21
Irving Wlk. RH10: Craw 2H 21
Irwin Dr. RH12: Hors 6E 29
Ivanhoe Cl. RH11: Craw 2G 15
Iveagh Cl. RH11: Craw 4F 21
Ivory Wlk. RH11: Craw 1B 20
Ivy Cl. RH13: Southw 4B 36
Ivydene Ind. Est. RH19: Ash W 1D 26
Ivy Dene La. RH19: Ash W 1D 26

J

Jackdaw Cl. RH11: Craw 3F 15
Jackdaw La. RH12: Hors 4A 30
Jackrells La. RH13: Southw 2D 36
Jackson Rd. RH11: Craw 5E 21
Jacobean Cl. RH10: Craw 6D 16
Jacobs Ct. RH10: Craw 4D 16
James Pl. RH10: Craw 6G 15
James Searle Ind. Est. RH12: Hors 5A 30
James Watt Way RH10: Craw 6B 10
Jarvis Cl. RH11: Craw 6D 14
Jasmine Ct. RH12: Hors 1G 33
Javelin Ct. RH10: Craw 2E 17
Jay Cl. RH13: Southw 3C 36
Jay Wlk. RH10: Turn H 6H 19
Jeans Ct. RH11: Craw 4E 21
Jengers La. RH14: Bill 2G 37
(off Jengers Mead)
Jengers Mead RH14: Bill 2G 37
Jengers Pas. RH14: Bill 2G 37
(off Jengers Mead)
Jenner Rd. RH10: Craw 6A 10
Jennings Way RH6: Horl 4A 6
Jersey Rd. RH11: Craw 3D 20
Jewel Wlk. RH11: Craw 2D 20
Jockey Mead RH12: Hors 2E 33
John Pound's Ho. RH11: Craw 1F 21
JOHNSON'S COMMON 1B 8
Johnson Wlk. RH10: Craw 2H 21
Molesfield Ct. RH11: Craw 2C 20
Jordans, The RH19: E Grin 5E 25
Jordans Ct. RH11: Craw 3G 15
Jordans Cres. RH11: Craw 2G 15
Jubilee Ct. RH14: Bill 3G 37
Jubilee Est. RH13: Hors 5A 30

Jubilee Wlk. RH10: Craw 5B 16
RH12: Hors 1G 33
(off Albion Way)
Judge's Ter. RH19: E Grin 5E 25
Juniper Rd. RH11: Craw 2F 15
Jura Cl. RH11: Craw 2E 21
Juxon Cl. RH11: Craw 1C 20

K

K2 Leisure Cen. 3G 21
Karenza Ct. RH13: Hors 6A 30
Keats Cl. RH12: Hors 2B 30
Keats Pl. RH19: E Grin 4D 24
Keble Cl. RH10: Craw 2E 17
KEEPER'S CORNER 3B 12
Keir Hardie Ho. RH11: Craw 4E 21
Kelmscott Ri. RH11: Craw 5E 21
Kelsey Cl. RH6: Horl 4E 5
Kelso Cl. RH10: Craw 4F 17
Kelvin Bus. Cen. RH10: Craw 2A 16
Kelvin La. RH10: Craw 1A 16
Kelvin Way RH10: Craw 1A 16
Kempshott M. RH12: Hors 5F 29
Kempshott Rd. RH12: Hors 5F 29
Kendale Cl. RH10: Craw 3D 22
Kenilworth Cl. RH11: Craw 3E 21
Kenilworth Pl. RH14: Bill 5F 37
Kenmara Cl. RH10: Craw 2B 16
Kenmara Ct. RH10: Craw 1B 16
Kennard Ct. RH18: F Row 4E 27
Kennedy Av. RH19: E Grin 2D 24
Kennedy Rd. RH13: Hors 2H 33
Kennel La. RH6: Hookw 5C 4
Kennet Cl. RH11: Craw 6C 14
Kensington Rd. RH11: Craw 3E 21
Kentwyns Dr. RH13: Hors 3A 34
Kentwyns Pl. RH13: Hors 3A 34
Kenya Ct. RH6: Horl 3E 5
Kerves La. RH13: Hors 6H 33
Kerwin Cl. RH13: Slinf 1A 32
Kestrel Cl. RH11: Craw 3F 15
RH12: Hors 4A 30
Kestrel Wlk. RH10: Turn H 6H 19
Keswick Cl. RH11: Ifield 1A 20
Keymer Rd. RH11: Craw 6F 15
Kidborough Rd. RH11: Craw 6C 14
KIDBROOKE PARK 6D 26
Kidbrooke Ri. RH18: F Row 5E 27
Kidmans Cl. RH12: Hors 4B 30
Kidworth Cl. RH6: Horl 2E 5
Kiln Cl. RH10: Craw D 4G 19
Kiln Heath Farm Bus. Cen.
RH6: Ship B 4H 11
Kiln Ho. RH19: E Grin 3D 24
(off Fosters Pl. E.)
Kiln La. RH6: Horl 2F 5
Kilnmead RH10: Craw 4G 15
Kilnmead Cl. RH10: Craw 4H 15
Kiln Rd. RH10: Craw D 4G 19
Kimberley Cl. RH6: Horl 4D 4
Kimberley Rd. RH10: Craw 4C 16
Kindersley Cl. RH19: E Grin 2H 25
King Edward Cl. RH13: Hors 5B 32
King Edward Rd. RH13: Hors 5B 32
Kingfisher Cl. RH10: Craw 1B 16
Kingfisher La. RH10: Turn H 6H 19
Kingfisher Ri. RH19: E Grin 5F 25
Kingfisher Way RH12: Hors 4G 29
King George Av. RH19: E Grin 2C 24
Kings Copse RH19: E Grin 5F 25
Kingscote Hill RH11: Craw 1E 21
King's Ct. RH13: Hors 6A 30
Kingsfold Cl. RH14: Bill 5G 37
Kings Ga. RH12: Hors 1F 33
Kingsgate RH10: Craw 5H 15
Kingsland Ct. RH10: Craw 5B 16
Kings La. RH13: Southw 1C 36
Kingslea RH13: Hors 6A 30
Kings Leisure Cen. 4E 25
Kingsley Cl. RH6: Horl 2E 5
Kingsley M. RH14: Bill 4G 37
Kingsley Rd. RH6: Horl 2E 5
RH11: Craw 2D 20
Kings Mead RH6: Smallf 4E 7
Kingsmead Cl. RH12: Hors 3D 30

Kingsmead Pl. RH12: Broadb H 6A 28
Kingsmead Rd. RH12: Broadb H 6B 28
Kings M. RH12: Hors 1F 33
Kings Pl. RH13: Hors 6A 30
Kings Rd. RH6: Horl 4F 5
RH13: Hors 6A 30
King St. RH19: E Grin 4E 25
Kingswood Cl. RH11: Craw 5F 21
Kipling Cl. RH10: Craw 3D 16
Kipling Ct. RH13: Hors 5C 30
Kipling Way RH19: E Grin 4C 24
Kirdford Cl. RH11: Craw 3D 14
Kites Cl. RH11: Craw 5F 15
Kithurst Cl. RH11: Craw 1G 21
Kitsbridge Ho. RH10: Copt 1H 17
(off Brookhill Rd.)
Kitsmead RH10: Copt 1H 17
Kittiwake Cl. RH11: Ifield 1A 20
Knepp Cl. RH10: Craw 5D 16
Knepp Ho. RH13: Hors 2H 33
(off Kennedy Rd.)
Knighton Cl. RH10: Craw 1E 17
Knob Hill RH12: Warnh 1D 28
Knole Cl. RH10: Craw 4E 17
Knole Gro. RH19: E Grin 2C 24
Knowle Cl. RH10: Copt 6B 12
Knowle Dr. RH10: Craw 6A 12

L

Laburnum Ct. (Caravan Pk.) RH6: Smallf . . .6F 7
Ladbroke Rd. RH6: Horl 2G 5
Lady Margaret Rd. RH11: Craw 4D 14
Lady Margaret Wlk. RH11: Craw 4D 14
Ladymead Cl. RH10: Craw 2D 22
Lake La. RH6: Horl 2H 5
Lakeside RH12: Hors 4G 29
Lakeside Dr. RH13: Southw 4C 36
Lake Vw. Rd. RH19: Felb 6G 13
Lamberhurst Wlk. RH10: Craw 6B 16
Lambeth Cl. RH11: Craw 3E 21
Lambeth Wlk. RH11: Craw 3E 21
Lamb Ho. RH13: Hors 6B 32
(off The Avenue)
Lambourn Cl. RH19: E Grin 2E 25
Lambourne Cl. RH10: Craw 1A 22
Lambs Cres. RH12: Hors 4B 30
Lambs Farm Cl. RH12: Hors 4C 30
Lambs Farm Rd. RH12: Hors 4B 30
Lambyn Cft. RH6: Horl 3H 5
Lampson Ct. RH10: Copt 6B 12
Lanark Cl. RH13: Hors 1A 34
Lancaster Cl. RH10: Craw 2E 17
Lancaster Dr. RH19: E Grin 2G 25
Lancelot Cl. RH11: Ifield 5B 14
Lancing Cl. RH11: Craw 3D 14
Lancing Ct. RH12: Hors 5C 30
Landen Pk. RH6: Horl 2D 4
Lanehurst Gdns. RH10: Craw 3D 16
Lanercost Rd. RH11: Craw 6F 15
Langdale Rd. RH11: Ifield 1A 20
Langhurstwood Rd. RH12: Hors 1G 29
Langley Dr. RH11: Craw 3F 15
LANGLEY GREEN 2F 15
LANGLEY GREEN HOSPITAL 1G 15
Langley La. RH11: Craw 3D 14
Langley Pde. RH11: Craw 2F 15
Langley Pl. RH11: Craw 2F 15
Langley Wlk. RH11: Craw 2E 15
Langridge Dr. RH19: E Grin 5E 25
Langridge Ho. RH12: Hors 1E 33
LANGSHOTT 3H 5
Langshott RH6: Horl 2G 5
Langshott La. RH6: Horl 4H 5
(not continuous)
Langstone Cl. RH10: Craw 2D 22
Lansbury Rd. RH11: Craw 3E 21
Lansdown Cl. RH12: Hors 3D 30
Lanyon Cl. RH12: Hors 3C 30
Lanyon M. RH12: Hors 3C 30
Lapwing Cl. RH13: Hors 6B 30
Larch End RH12: Hors 6F 29
Larches, The RH12: Hors 3E 31
RH19: E Grin 1H 25

Larches Ho. RH19: E Grin 1H 25
Larches Way RH10: Craw D 3G 19
Larkfield Ct. RH6: Smallf 4D 6
Larkins Rd. RH6: Gatw 2G 9
Lark Ri. RH10: Turn H 6H 19
   RH11: Craw 3F 15
Larksfield RH6: Horl 3G 5
Larkspur Way RH13: Southw 2C 36
Larks Vw. RH14: Bill 3F 37
Lashmere RH10: Copt 6C 12
Laski Ct. RH11: Craw 4E 21
Latimer Cl. RH11: Craw 2G 15
Laud Dr. RH10: Craw 6E 17
Laughton Rd. RH12: Hors 4B 30
Laundry Cotts. RH11: Craw 3C 20
Laurel Cl. RH10: Craw 2B 22
Laurel Dene RH19: E Grin 4F 25
Laurels, The RH10: Craw 2B 16
   RH13: Southw 3B 36
Laurel Wlk. RH13: Hors 2B 34
Lavant Cl. RH11: Craw 6C 14
Lavington Cl. RH11: Craw 4C 14
Lawrence Cl. RH10: Craw 1E 23
Laws Cl. RH11: Ifield 6B 14
Lawson Hunt Ind. Pk. RH12: Broadb H . . .5B 28
Lea Cl. RH11: Craw 6C 14
Leacroft RH19: E Grin 3D 24
Lechford Rd. RH6: Horl 5F 5
Leechpool La. RH13: Hors 5C 30
Leeds RH13: Southw 3C 36
Lee St. RH6: Horl 4D 4
Leggyfield Ct. RH12: Hors 4F 29
Leicester Ct. RH10: Craw 5E 17
Leigh-Hunt Ho. RH13: Hors 6C 32
   (off The Avenue)
Leighlands RH10: Craw 3D 16
Leisure Pursuits 1E 27
Leith Vw. Rd. RH10: Craw 4C 30
Le May Cl. RH6: Horl 3F 5
Lemmington Way RH12: Hors 2B 30
Leonardslee Ct. RH10: Craw 1C 22
Leonard Way RH13: Hors 1B 34
Leopold Rd. RH11: Craw 5F 15
Letchworth Ct. RH11: Craw 2B 20
Leveret La. RH11: Craw 3E 15
Lewes Cl. RH10: Craw 5D 16
Lewes Rd. RH18: F Row 6E 27
   RH19: Ash W, E Grin, F Row
   . . . . .5F 25 & 1C 26
Lewisham Cl. RH11: Craw 3F 21
Leybourne Av. RH11: Craw 4F 21
Leybourne Pl. RH19: Felb 6B 24
Lidsey Cl. RH10: Craw 1D 22
Lime Av. RH12: Hors 5C 30
Lime Cl. RH10: Copt 6A 12
   RH11: Craw 2F 15
Lime Kiln Rd. RH13: Mann H 5E 35
Limes, The RH12: Hors 5G 29
   (off Trafalgar Rd.)
   RH19: Felb 1A 24
Limes Av. RH6: Horl 5G 5
Linchmere Pl. RH11: Craw 4D 14
Lincoln Cl. RH6: Horl 5F 5
   RH10: Craw 2H 21
Linden Av. RH19: E Grin 3C 24
Linden Cl. RH10: Craw 2B 22
   RH12: Hors 5A 30
Lindens, The RH10: Copt 6A 12
Lindgren Wlk. RH11: Craw 4E 21
Lindisfarne Ho. RH11: Craw 1E 21
   (off St Aidan Cl.)
Lines Cl. RH18: F Row 5H 27
Lingfield Dr. RH10: Craw 4F 17
Lingfield Rd. RH19: E Grin 1D 24
Link, The RH11: Craw 5G 15
   (not continuous)
Link 10 RH10: Craw 2A 16
Linnell Cl. RH11: Craw 5E 21
Linnett Cl. RH10: Turn H 6H 19
Lintott Sq. RH13: Southw 4B 36
   (off Fairbank Rd.)
Lintott Gdns. RH13: Hors 6A 30
Lismore Cres. RH11: Craw 2E 21
Lit. Bridges Cl. RH13: Southw 4B 36
Little Cl. RH13: Southw 6B 36
Little Comptons RH13: Hors 1B 34
Little Crabtree RH11: Craw 4F 15

Lit. East St. RH14: Bill 2G 37
Little Grebe RH12: Hors 4G 29
Little Hatch RH12: Hors 4B 30
LITTLE HAVEN .4A 30
Littlehaven Station (Rail) 4B 30
Lit. King St. RH19: E Grin 4E 25
Little Oaks RH19: E Grin 2D 24
   (off Springfield)
Lit. Park Enterprises RH11: Ifield 6B 8
Littlehaven La. RH12: Hors 4B 30
Livingstone Rd. RH10: Craw 1H 21
   RH13: Hors 2H 33
Lloyds Ct. RH10: Craw 2H 15
Lockwood Cl. RH11: Craw 4C 30
Lockwood Ct. RH10: Craw 3A 16
Lodge Cl. RH11: Craw 5F 15
   RH19: E Grin 4C 24
Lodge Wlk. RH6: Horl 4E 5
   (off Thornton Pl.)
London Flds. Ho. RH11: Craw 4F 21
LONDON GATWICK AIRPORT
   North Terminal 1H 9
   South Terminal 2B 10
London Rd. RH10: Craw, Low H 4G 15
   RH11: Craw 3G 15
   RH12: Hors 1G 33
   RH17: Bal .6G 23
   RH18: F Row 3E 27
   RH19: E Grin 1A 24
Lone Oak RH6: Smallf 6E 7
Long Acre RH10: Craw D 3F 19
Longbridge Ga. RH6: Gatw 1H 9
   (off Arrivals Rd.)
Longbridge Rd. RH6: Horl 6E 5
Longbridge Rdbt. RH6: Horl 5D 4
Longbridge Wlk. RH6: Horl 6E 5
Longbridge Way RH6: Gatw 6E 5
Longchamps Cl. RH6: Horl 4H 5
Long Cl. RH10: Craw 5E 17
Longfellow Cl. RH12: Hors 2A 30
Longfield Rd. RH12: Hors 3E 33
Longhurst Rd. RH11: Craw 4D 20
Long Mdw. Vs. RH6: Charlw 4B 8
Longmere Rd. RH10: Craw 3G 15
Longwall RH19: E Grin 1A 24
Longwood Vw. RH10: Craw 2B 22
Longyard Ho. RH6: Horl 2G 5
Loppets Rd. RH10: Craw 1A 22
Loriners RH10: Craw 2G 21
Loveletts RH11: Craw 6D 14
Lovell Path RH11: Ifield 6B 14
Lovers La. RH13: Hors 5G 33
Lowdell's Cl. RH19: E Grin 1C 24
Lowdells Dr. RH19: E Grin 1C 24
Lowdells La. RH19: E Grin 1B 24
Lowe Cl. RH11: Craw 5E 21
Lwr. Barn Cl. RH12: Hors 4B 30
Lower Dene RH19: E Grin 4G 25
Lower Mere RH19: E Grin 5F 25
Lower Rd. RH18: F Row 4F 27
Lower Sq. RH18: F Row 4F 27
Lwr. Station Rd. RH14: Bill 5G 37
Lwr. Tanbridge Way RH12: Hors 1F 33
Lowestoft Wlk. RH10: Craw 1C 22
LOWFIELD HEATH 4H 9
Lowfield Heath Rd. RH6: Charlw 3C 8
Lowfield Heath Rdbt. RH10: Low H 5H 9
   (off London Rd.)
Lowfield Way RH11: Low H 4H 9
Loxwood Wlk. RH11: Craw 3C 14
   (not continuous)
Lucas Cl. RH10: Craw 2C 22
   RH19: E Grin 4G 25
Lucas Rd. RH12: Warnh 1C 28
Lucerne Dr. RH10: Craw 2E 23
Luggs Cl. RH14: Bill 3G 37
Lulworth Cl. RH11: Craw 2D 20
Lumley Ct. RH6: Horl 3F 5
Lumley Rd. RH6: Horl 3F 5
Lundy Cl. RH11: Craw 2F 21
Lutyens Cl. RH11: Craw 1B 20
Luxford Cl. RH12: Hors 4B 30
Luxford's La. RH19: E Grin 2B 26
Luxford Way RH14: Bill 4F 37
Lydon Ho. RH11: Craw 2G 15
Lyndhurst Cl. RH11: Craw 6G 15
Lyndhurst Farm Cl. RH19: Felb 6A 14

Lynton Cl. RH19: E Grin 3F 25
Lynton Pk. Av. RH19: E Grin 3F 25
Lynwood Ct. RH12: Hors 6G 29
Lyon Cl. RH10: Craw 3D 22
Lyon Ct. RH13: Hors 1A 34
Lyric Cl. RH11: Craw 1E 23
Lytton Dr. RH10: Craw 4E 17

M

McIndoe Rd. RH19: E Grin 2D 24
MCINDOE SURGICAL CENTRE 2F 25
McIver Cl. RH19: Felb 6B 24
Macleod Rd. RH13: Hors 2A 34
   (not continuous)
Maddox Dr. RH10: Worth 6E 17
Madehurst Cl. RH11: Craw 2C 20
Madeira Av. RH12: Hors 1G 33
Magdalene Cl. RH10: Craw 2D 16
Magellan Ter. RH10: Craw 1B 16
Magistrates' Court
   Crawley 5H 15
   Horsham .6G 29
Magnolia Ct. RH6: Horl 4F 5
Magpie Wlk. RH10: Craw 3A 16
MAIDENBOWER 1D 22
Maidenbower Bus. Pk. RH10: Worth 1F 23
Maidenbower Community Sports Cen. . . .1C 22
Maidenbower Dr. RH10: Craw 1D 22
Maidenbower La. RH10: Craw 6D 16
   (Blackett Rd.)
   RH10: Craw 1C 22
   (Marion Rd.)
Maidenbower Pl. RH10: Craw 1D 22
Maidenbower Sq. RH10: Craw 1D 22
Maiden La. RH11: Craw 3F 15
Maine Ho. RH13: Hors 6C 32
   (off The Avenue)
Maize Cft. RH6: Horl 3H 5
Major's Hill RH10: Worth 6B 18
Malcolm Gdns. RH6: Hookw 6C 4
Malham Cl. RH10: Craw 2D 22
Mallard Cl. RH6: Horl 2F 5
   RH12: Hors 4G 29
Mallard Pl. RH19: E Grin 5F 25
Mallow Cl. RH12: Hors 3A 30
Malthouse Rd. RH10: Craw 1G 21
Maltings, The RH14: Bill 2G 37
   (off High St.)
Malvern Rd. RH11: Craw 6F 15
Mann Cl. RH11: Craw 5E 21
Manning Cl. RH19: E Grin 2D 24
Mannings Cl. RH10: Craw 2E 17
MANNINGS HEATH 5E 35
Mannings Heath Golf Course 4G 35
Manor Cl. RH6: Horl 4E 5
Manor Ct. RH10: Craw 2A 16
   RH12: Hors 4C 30
Manor Dr. RH6: Horl 4E 5
Manor Flds. RH13: Hors 5C 30
Manorfields RH11: Craw 3A 20
Manor Ga. RH10: Craw 2A 16
Manor La. RH13: Hors 3D 34
Manor Rd. RH12: Hors 4C 30
   RH19: E Grin 3C 24
Manor Royal RH10: Craw 2H 15
Mnr. Royal Ind. Est. RH10: Craw 2H 15
Manor Wlk. RH6: Horl 4E 5
   (off Manor Dr.)
Maple Cl. RH11: Craw 2F 15
   RH12: Hors 4C 30
   RH14: Bill 3F 37
Mapledown RH13: Southw 3B 36
Maple Dr. RH19: E Grin 4G 25
Maple Grn. RH11: Craw 6F 15
Maplehurst Cl. RH14: Bill 4H 37
Maple Rd. RH14: Bill 4H 37
Mardens, The RH11: Craw 4E 15
Marion Rd. RH10: Craw 1C 22
Marjoram Ct. RH6: Horl 2H 5
   (off Newman Rd.)
Market House, The RH19: E Grin 4F 25
   (off Cantelupe Rd.)
Market Sq. RH12: Hors 2G 33
Marlborough Cl. RH11: Craw 3F 21
   RH12: Hors 4H 29

Marlborough Pl. *RH12: Hors* 6F **29**
(off Rushams Rd.)
Marlow Ct. RH10: Craw 4G **15**
Marlpit Cl. RH19: E Grin 2E **25**
Marringdean Rd. RH14: Bill 5G **37**
Marshall Rd. RH10: Craw 1D **22**
Marsh Ct. RH11: Craw 4E **21**
Martin Cl. RH11: Craw 3G **15**
Martins, The RH10: Craw D 3H **19**
Martlets, The RH10: Craw 5H **15**
Martlets Cl. RH12: Hors 4G **29**
Martyns Pl. RH19: E Grin 5F **25**
Martyrs Av. RH11: Craw 2F **15**
Marvell Cl. RH10: Craw 3D **16**
Masefield Rd. RH11: Craw 2B **20**
Mason Cl. RH19: E Grin 3E **25**
Mason Rd. RH10: Craw 1H **21**
Masons Fld. RH13: Mann H 5E **35**
Massetts Rd. RH6: Horl 5E **5**
Matthews Dr. RH10: Craw 3C **22**
Matthey Pl. RH10: Craw 2E **17**
Maunsell Pk. RH10: Craw 5C **16**
Maxton Wlk. RH11: Craw 4E **21**
Maxwell Way RH10: Craw 2B **16**
Mayes Cl. RH10: Craw 6D **16**
Mayfield RH10: Worth 5E **17**
Mayflower Cl. RH10: Craw 6E **17**
Maynard Cl. RH10: Copt 5B **12**
Maypole Rd. RH19: Ash W 1E **27**
  RH19: E Grin 3D **24**
Meadow, The RH10: Copt 6H **11**
Meadow App. RH10: Copt 6H **11**
Meadowbrook Ind. Cen.
  RH10: Craw .2B **16**
Meadow Cl. RH10: Copt 6H **11**
  RH12: Hors .4C **30**
Meadow Ct. RH19: E Grin 3E **25**
Meadowcroft Cl. RH6: Horl 1D **10**
  RH11: Craw .6C **14**
  RH19: E Grin 3C **24**
Meadow Farm La. RH10: Craw 2B **30**
Meadowgate *RH12: Hors* **2B 30**
(off Giblets La.)
Meadowlands RH11: Craw 5F **15**
Meadowside RH6: Horl 3G **5**
Meadow Vw. RH6: Smallf 4F **7**
Meadow Way RH6: Horl 2H **5**
Mead Pl. RH6: Smallf 4F **7**
Mead Rd. RH10: Craw 4H **15**
Meads, The RH19: E Grin 6E **25**
Meadvale RH12: Hors 1D **32**
Meadway, The RH6: Horl 4H **5**
Meath Gdns. RH10: Craw 2D **4**
MEATH GREEN 2E **5**
Meath Grn. Av. RH6: Horl 2E **5**
Meath Grn. La. RH6: Horl 1D **4**
Medlar Cl. RH11: Craw 2F **15**
Medway RH10: Turn H 6F **19**
Medway Ct. RH12: Hors 4D **30**
Medway Dr. RH18: F Row 5G **27**
Medway Rd. RH11: Craw 6C **14**
Medway Vw. RH18: F Row 5G **27**
Medwin Wlk. RH12: Hors 1G **33**
Melbourne Way RH12: Hors 4B **30**
Melksham Cl. RH13: Hors 2A **34**
Memorial Gdns. 5H **15**
Mendip Wlk. RH11: Craw 5E **15**
Mercer Cl. RH10: Craw 2D **22**
Mercer Rd. RH12: Hors 1G **29**
Mercury Cl. RH11: Craw 2B **20**
Mereworth Dr. RH10: Craw 3E **17**
Meridian Cl. RH11: Craw 2C **20**
Meridian Gro. RH6: Horl 3H **5**
Meridian Way RH19: E Grin 2F **25**
Merlin Cen. RH11: Craw 6G **9**
Merlin Cl. RH11: Ifield 5B **14**
Merlin Way RH19: E Grin 2G **25**
Merryfield Dr. RH12: Hors 1E **33**
Merton Rd. RH11: Craw 5E **21**
Messenger Cl. RH11: Craw 3D **14**
Metana Ho. RH10: Craw 6B **10**
Metcalf Way RH11: Craw 1G **15**
Mews, The *RH12: Broadb H* **5B 28**
(off Old Guildford Rd.)
Michael Cres. RH6: Horl 6F **5**
Michael Flds. RH18: F Row 5E **27**
Michell Cl. RH12: Hors 1E **33**

Mick Mill's Race RH13: Colg 5H **31**
Middlefield RH6: Horl 3H **5**
Middle Row RH19: E Grin 5F **25**
Middle St. RH12: Hors 1G **33**
Middleton Ho. *RH13: Hors* **5B 32**
(off The Avenue)
Middleton Rd. RH12: Hors 1E **33**
Middleton Way RH11: Ifield 6B **14**
Midgeley Rd. RH10: Craw 3A **16**
Midhurst Cl. RH11: Craw 4D **14**
Milborne Rd. RH10: Craw 3D **22**
Millais RH13: Hors 6C **30**
Millais Cl. RH11: Craw 3C **20**
Millais Ct. RH13: Hors 5C **30**
Millbank, The RH11: Craw 5C **14**
Mill Bay La. RH12: Hors 2F **33**
Mill Cl. RH6: Horl 3D **4**
  RH19: E Grin 6E **25**
Mill Cotts. RH19: E Grin 6E **25**
Mill Ct. RH10: Craw 6A **16**
Millennium Ho. *RH11: Craw* **2C 20**
(off Meridian Cl.)
Millers Ga. RH12: Hors 4H **29**
Mill Farm Rd. RH13: Hors 5H **31**
Millfield RH13: Southw 5C **36**
Millfield Cl. RH11: Craw 4E **15**
Millfields Cres. RH6: Charlw 3A **8**
Mill La. RH6: Hookw 4C **4**
  RH10: Copt .6D **12**
  RH11: Ifield .3D **14**
  RH13: Itch 3A **32**
  RH14: Bill 3G **37**
  RH19: Felb 6A **24**
Mill Rd. RH10: Craw 4C **16**
Mills Cl. RH13: Hors 2B **34**
Mill Straight RH13: Southw 5B **36**
Millthorpe Rd. RH12: Hors 5B **30**
Mill Way RH14: Bill 2F **37**
(not continuous)
  RH19: E Grin 6E **25**
Milne Cl. RH11: Craw 2B **20**
Milnwood Rd. RH12: Hors 6G **29**
Milton Cres. RH19: E Grin 5C **24**
Milton Mt. RH10: Craw 2E **17**
Milton Mt. Av. RH10: Craw 3D **16**
Milton Mount Gdns. 2E **17**
Milton Rd. RH10: Craw 4D **16**
  RH12: Hors .6G **29**
Mindelheim Av. RH19: E Grin 3H **25**
Miranda Wlk. RH11: Craw 1B **20**
Mistley Gdns. RH6: Hookw 5C **4**
Mitchells Rd. RH10: Craw 5A **16**
Mitford Wlk. RH11: Craw 2D **20**
Mitre Cl. RH12: Hors 1F **33**
Moat Rd. RH19: E Grin 3E **25**
Moat Wlk. RH10: Craw 4D **16**
Mole Cl. RH11: Craw 3E **15**
Molins Ct. *RH11: Craw* **2D 20**
(off Brideake Cl.)
Monarch Cl. RH11: Craw 2D **20**
Monksfield RH10: Craw 5A **16**
Montreux Ct. RH11: Craw 5E **15**
Moons La. RH13: Hors 2A **34**
Moorcroft Cl. RH11: Craw 4E **15**
Moore Ct. RH12: Hors 2E **33**
Moorhead Rd. RH13: Hors 4D **30**
Moorhead Rdbt. RH12: Hors 2D **30**
Moorings, The RH19: E Grin 2A **24**
Moorland Rd. RH10: Craw 2D **22**
Moor Pk. RH6: Horl 5G **5**
(off Aurum Cl.)
Moor Pk. Cres. RH11: Ifield 6A **14**
Moor Pl. RH19: E Grin 3D **24**
Morecambe Cl. RH11: Craw 1C **20**
Morgan Ho. *RH10: Craw* **4C 16**
(off Trafalgar Gdns.)
Morrell Av. RH12: Hors 4B **30**
Morris Dr. RH14: Bill 4E **37**
Morrison Ct. RH11: Craw 4E **21**
Morth Gdns. RH12: Hors 2G **33**
Morton Cl. RH11: Craw 5E **21**
Morton Rd. RH19: E Grin 6E **25**
Mosford Cl. RH6: Horl 2E **5**
Mountbatten Cl. RH11: Craw 3F **21**
Mount Cl. RH10: Craw 4E **17**
Mount Noddy .3E **25**
Mowbray Dr. RH11: Craw 1C **20**

Moyne Rd. RH11: Craw 3F **21**
Muirfield Cl. RH11: Ifield 6A **14**
Mulberry Cl. RH12: Hors 4G **29**
Mulberry Gdns. RH12: Broadb H 6C **28**
Mulberry Ga. RH19: Felb 1A **24**
Mulberry Rd. RH11: Craw 2E **15**
Mullein Wlk. RH11: Craw 3D **20**
Murray Ct. RH11: Craw 4D **20**
  RH13: Hors .5D **30**
Musgrave Av. RH19: E Grin 6E **25**
Myrtle La. RH14: Bill 4G **37**

N

Naldrett Cl. RH12: Hors 5B **30**
Napier Way RH10: Craw 2A **16**
Nash Rd. RH10: Craw 2H **21**
Natts La. RH14: Bill 4F **37**
Neale Cl. RH19: E Grin 2B **24**
Needles Cl. RH12: Hors 2F **33**
Nelson Cl. RH10: Craw 6D **16**
Nelson Rd. RH12: Hors 6F **29**
Neptune Cl. RH11: Craw 1B **20**
Nesbit Ct. RH11: Craw 2B **20**
Netherton Cl. RH13: Southw 1B **36**
Netherwood RH11: Craw 1E **21**
Netley Cl. RH11: Craw 5F **21**
Nevile Cl. RH11: Craw 2D **20**
Newark Rd. RH10: Craw 3A **16**
Newbridge Cl. RH12: Broadb H 6A **28**
Newbridge Rd. RH14: Bill 3E **37**
(not continuous)
Newbridge Rd. E. RH14: Bill 3F **37**
Newbridge Rd. W. RH14: Bill 3E **37**
New Bridge Rdbt. RH12: Broadb H 6A **28**
Newbury Rd. RH10: Craw 5E **17**
Newfield Ho. *RH11: Craw* **4F 21**
(off Kensington Rd.)
NEWFOUND OUT 1D **36**
Newhouse Bus. Cen.
  RH12: Fay 2E **31**
Newlands Cl. RH6: Horl 2E **5**
Newlands Cres. RH19: E Grin 3D **24**
Newlands Pk. RH10: Copt 6D **12**
Newlands Pl. RH18: F Row 4F **27**
Newlands Rd. RH11: Craw 6F **15**
  RH12: Hors .5G **29**
Newman Cl. RH10: Craw 1D **22**
Newman Rd. RH6: Horl 2H **5**
Newmarket Rd. RH10: Craw 2B **22**
New Moorhead Dr. RH12: Hors 3E **31**
New Rd. RH6: Smallf 4E **7**
  RH13: Southw 1B **36**
  RH14: Bill 1H **37**
Newstead Hall RH6: Horl 5A **6**
New St. RH10: Craw 4B **16**
  RH13: Hors .2H **33**
Newton Rd. RH10: Craw 1A **16**
NEW TOWN 2H **33**
New Town RH10: Copt 6A **12**
Newtown Ct. RH13: Hors 2H **33**
NHS WALK-IN CENTRE
  Crawley 5F **15**
(within Crawley Hospital)
Nightingale Cl. RH11: Craw 3F **15**
  RH19: E Grin 6D **24**
Nightingale Ind. Est.
  RH12: Hors .6H **29**
Nightingale La. RH10: Turn H 6H **19**
Nightingale Rd. RH12: Hors 6H **29**
Nightingales Cl. RH13: Hors 1B **34**
Nightingale Wlk. RH14: Bill 3G **37**
Nimrod Ct. *RH10: Craw* **4E 16**
(off Wakehams Grn. Dr.)
Ninfield Ct. RH11: Craw 3C **20**
Niven Cl. RH10: Craw 6E **17**
Nokes Ct. RH10: Craw 6A **16**
Norfolk Cl. RH6: Horl 5F **5**
  RH11: Craw .3B **20**
Norfolk Ct. RH12: Hors 4D **30**
Norfolk Rd. RH12: Hors 1H **33**
Norfolk Ter. RH12: Hors 1H **33**
Norman Cl. RH14: Bill 2H **37**
Normandy RH12: Hors 2G **33**
Normandy Cl. RH10: Craw 1C **22**
  RH19: E Grin 5F **25**

Normandy Gdns. RH12: Hors 2G 33
Normanhurst Cl. RH10: Craw 5A 16
Normans Gdns. RH19: E Grin 4E 25
Norman's Rd. RH1: Out 2F 7
  RH6: Out, Smallf 2F 7
North Ash RH12: Hors 5G 29
North Cl. RH10: Craw 4A 16
Northdown Cl. RH12: Hors 5B 30
Northdown Ter. RH19: E Grin 2D 24
NORTH END .2B 24
North End RH19: E Grin 2B 24
NORTHGATE 4H 15
Northgate Av. RH10: Craw 5H 15
Northgate Pl. RH10: Craw 4H 15
Northgate Rd. RH6: Gatw 1A 10
  (off Racecourse Rd.)
  RH10: Craw 5G 15
Nth. Heath Cl. RH12: Hors 4H 29
Nth. Heath Est. RH12: Hors 3H 29
Nth. Heath La. RH12: Hors 5H 29
Nth. Holmes Cl. RH12: Hors 4D 30
Northlands Rd. RH12: Hors 2A 30
North Mead RH12: Hors 3H 15
North Pde. RH12: Hors 4G 29
Nth. Perimeter Rd. RH6: Gatw 3G 9
  (off Old Control Tower Rd.)
North Rd. RH10: Craw 3B 16
North St. RH10: Turn H 6F 19
  RH12: Hors 1H 33
Nth. Terminal App. RH6: Gatw 1A 10
Northway RH6: Gatw 1A 10
Northwood Pk. RH10: Craw 1B 16
Norwich Rd. RH10: Craw 1C 22
Norwood Hill Rd. RH6: Charlw, Nor H 2B 8
Nuffield Health Club
  Crawley 4G 17
Nurserylands RH11: Craw 5D 14
Nursery La. RH6: Hookw 5C 4
Nutbourne Ct. RH12: Hors 4H 29
  (off Woodstock Cl.)
Nutham La. RH13: Southw 4C 36
Nuthatch Way RH10: Turn H 6H 19
  RH12: Hors 2H 29
Nuthurst Cl. RH11: Craw 4D 14
Nuyuu Fitness
  East Grinstead 4E 25
Nyes La. RH13: Southw 2B 36
Nymans Cl. RH12: Hors 2C 30
Nymans Cl. RH10: Craw 2C 22

O

Oakapple Cl. RH11: Craw 4E 21
Oak Cl. RH10: Copt 6H 11
  RH13: Southw 6B 36
Oak Ct. RH10: Craw 1G 15
  RH19: E Grin 3D 24
  (off Newlands Cres.)
Oak Cft. RH19: E Grin 5G 25
Oak Dell RH10: Craw 4D 16
Oak Farm Pl. RH19: Felb 6B 24
Oakfield Ct. RH6: Horl 4F 5
  (off Consort Way)
Oakfields RH10: Craw 3E 17
Oakfield Way RH19: E Grin 2F 25
Oakhaven RH10: Craw 1G 21
OAKHILL 2A 34
Oakhill Chase RH10: Craw 4E 17
Oakhill Rd. RH13: Hors 1A 34
Oak Ho. RH10: Craw 1G 15
Oakhurst Bus. Pk.
  RH13: Southw 1C 36
Oakhurst Gdns. RH19: E Grin 3C 24
Oakhurst M. RH13: Hors 5C 30
Oakland Cl. RH13: Hors 3A 34
Oaklands RH6: Horl 4H 5
  RH12: Hors 4F 29
  RH13: Hors 1A 34
  RH14: Bill .4G 37
Oak La. RH12: Broadb H 6C 28
Oakleigh Rd. RH12: Hors 5B 30
Oakley Cl. RH19: E Grin 6H 25
Oak Rd. RH11: Craw 6F 15
  RH13: Southw 4A 36
Oaks, The RH13: Southw 3B 36
  RH19: E Grin 5G 25

Oaks Cl. RH12: Hors 3D 30
Oakside Ct. RH6: Horl 3H 5
Oakside La. RH6: Horl 3H 5
Oak Tree Cl. RH19: E Grin 2C 24
Oak Tree Way RH13: Hors 5B 30
Oak Way RH10: Craw 4H 15
  RH13: Mann H 5E 35
Oakwood Ct. RH11: Craw 5E 21
  (off Mann Cl.)
Oakwood Ind. Pk. RH10: Craw 2B 16
Oakwood Pk. RH18: F Row 5F 27
Oakwood Rd. RH6: Horl 3F 5
Oakwood Sports Cen. 4H 5
Oates Wlk. RH10: Craw 2A 22
Oatlands RH6: Horl 3H 5
  RH11: Craw 6D 14
Oberon Way RH11: Craw 2B 20
Observer Ct. RH12: Hors 2G 33
Old Brighton Rd. RH11: Pease P 6E 21
Old Brighton Rd. Sth.
  RH11: Low H 5H 9
Oldbury Cl. RH12: Hors 2C 30
Old Control Twr. Rd. RH6: Gatw 3G 9
Old Convent RH19: E Grin 3E 25
Old Crawley Rd. RH12: Fay 3E 31
Old Denne Gdns. RH12: Hors 2G 33
Old Dorking Rd. RH12: Warnh 3F 29
Oldfield Cl. RH6: Horl 6E 5
Oldfield Rd. RH6: Horl 6E 5
Old Guildford Rd. RH12: Broadb H 5B 28
Old Holbrook RH12: Hors 1A 30
Old Hollow RH10: Craw, Worth 5G 17
Old Horsham Rd. RH11: Craw 1E 21
Old House M. RH12: Hors 1G 33
Old Manor Cl. RH11: Craw 3D 14
Old Manor Ct. RH11: Craw 3D 14
Old Martyrs RH11: Craw 2G 15
Old Millmeads RH12: Hors 4G 29
Old Orchards RH10: Worth 5F 17
Old Overthorpe RH6: Smallf 6E 7
Old Post Cotts. RH12: Broadb H 6C 28
  (off Wickhurst La.)
Old Pound Cotts. RH11: Ifield 4A 14
Old Rd. RH19: E Grin 4F 25
Old Station Cl. RH10: Craw D 4G 19
Old Wickhurst La.
  RH12: Broadb H 2B 32
Oliver Rd. RH12: Hors 6E 29
Olivier Rd. RH10: Craw 6E 17
Onslow Ct. RH10: Craw 2B 16
Ontario Cl. RH6: Smallf 5D 6
Orchard, The RH6: Horl 4F 5
  RH12: Broadb H 6B 28
  RH13: Hors 5D 30
Orchard Ct. RH6: Horl 3E 5
Orchard Cotts. RH6: Charlw 2C 8
Orchard Dr. RH6: Horl 2G 5
Orchard Gdns. RH12: Hors 5G 29
Orchard Rd. RH6: Smallf 4F 7
  RH13: Hors 2A 34
Orchards, The RH11: Ifield 6A 14
  RH12: Hors 4B 30
Orchard St. RH11: Craw 5G 15
Orchard Way RH19: E Grin 4E 25
Orde Cl. RH10: Craw 2E 17
Oriel, The RH6: Horl 5F 5
Oriel Cl. RH11: Craw 2D 16
Orion Ct. RH11: Craw 1A 20
Ormesby Wlk. RH10: Craw 1C 22
Osborne Cl. RH11: Craw 3E 21
Osmund Cl. RH10: Worth 5F 17
Osmund Cl. RH14: Bill 2G 37
Osney Cl. RH11: Craw 6F 15
Ostlers Vw. RH14: Bill 4F 37
Otford Cl. RH11: Craw 5F 21
Otterbourne Pl. RH19: E Grin 4B 24
Otway Cl. RH11: Craw 1C 20
Oulton Wlk. RH10: Craw 1C 22
Overdene Dr. RH11: Craw 5D 14
Overton Ct. RH19: E Grin 4E 25
Overton Shaw RH19: E Grin 1E 25
Owers Cl. RH13: Hors 1A 34
Owlbeech Ct. RH13: Hors 5D 30
Owlbeech Pl. RH13: Hors 5D 30
Owlbeech Way RH13: Hors 5D 30
Owletts RH10: Craw 4E 17
Owlscastle Cl. RH12: Hors 4H 29

Oxford Rd. RH10: Craw 3H 21
  RH13: Hors 1H 33

P

Packer Cl. RH19: E Grin 1G 25
Paddock, The RH10: Craw 4E 17
Paddock Gdns. RH19: E Grin 6E 25
Paddockhurst Rd. RH10: Turn H 5G 23
  RH11: Craw 6D 14
  RH17: Turn H 5G 23
Padstow Wlk. RH11: Craw 1B 20
Padwick Rd. RH13: Hors 1C 34
Page Ct. RH10: Craw 6A 16
  RH13: Hors 2H 33
Paget Cl. RH13: Hors 3A 34
PAGEWOOD .2A 8
Pagewood Cl. RH10: Craw 1E 23
Pallingham Dr. RH10: Craw 2D 22
Palmer Cl. RH6: Horl 2E 5
Palmer Rd. RH10: Craw 2D 22
Pankhurst Cl. RH11: Craw 4E 21
Pannell Cl. RH19: E Grin 5D 24
Parade, The RH10: Craw 4H 15
  RH12: Hors 6E 29
  (off Cootes Av.)
  RH19: E Grin 2B 24
PARBROOK 4F 37
Parham Rd. RH11: Craw 4C 14
Parish Ho. RH11: Craw 6G 15
Parish La. RH10: Pease P . . . . . .6F 21 & 6A 22
Park & Ride
  Hop Oast (Horsham) 5E 33
Park Cres. RH18: F Row 5G 27
Parker Cl. RH10: Craw 6E 17
Park Farm Cl. RH12: Hors 2H 29
Park Farm Rd. RH12: Hors 2H 29
Parkfield RH12: Hors 6G 29
Parkfield Cl. RH11: Craw 6C 14
Parkhurst Gro. RH6: Horl 3D 4
Parkhurst Rd. RH6: Horl 3D 4
Park La. RH19: Ash W, E Grin 1D 26
Parklawn Av. RH6: Horl 2E 5
Park Pl. RH12: Hors 2G 33
Park Ri. RH12: Hors 5F 29
Park Rd. RH6: Smallf 6F 7
  RH18: F Row 5G 27
  RH19: E Grin 4D 24
Parkside RH10: Craw 5H 15
  RH19: E Grin 4C 24
Parkside M. RH12: Hors 1H 33
Park St. RH12: Hors 1H 33
Park Ter. Courtyard RH12: Hors 2H 33
  (off Park Ter.)
Park Ter. E. RH13: Hors 2H 33
Park Ter. W. RH13: Hors 2H 33
Park Vw. RH6: Horl 4F 5
  RH11: Craw 6F 15
Park Vw. Gdns. RH19: E Grin 2D 24
Park Way RH6: Horl 3D 16
  RH12: Hors 1G 33
Parnell Cl. RH10: Craw 1E 23
Parry Cl. RH13: Hors 5E 31
Parsonage Bus. Pk. RH11: Craw 5A 30
Parsonage Farm Ind. Est. RH12: Hors 4A 30
Parsonage Rd. RH12: Hors 5H 29
Parsonage Way RH12: Hors 5A 30
Parsons Cl. RH6: Smallf 3D 4
Parsons Wlk. RH12: Hors 3D 32
Parthings La. RH13: Hors 4C 32
Partridge Pl. RH10: Turn H 5H 19
Pasture, The RH10: Craw 5D 16
Patching Cl. RH11: Craw 4C 14
Patchings RH13: Hors 6B 30
Path Link RH10: Craw 4H 15
Patrington Cl. RH11: Craw 2D 20
Patterdale Cl. RH11: Craw 1E 21
Pavement, The RH10: Craw 5H 17
Pavilions, The RH10: Worth 4F 17
Pavilions in the Park, The 6G 29
Pavilion Way RH19: E Grin 5E 25
Pax Cl. RH11: Craw 1B 20
Payne Cl. RH10: Craw 3E 17
Peacemaker Cl. RH11: Craw 1B 20
Peacock Wlk. RH11: Craw 2D 20

Pearson Rd. RH10: Craw 4D 16
Peary Cl. RH12: Hors 3H 29
PEASE POTTAGE 6F 21
Pease Pottage Golf Course 6D 20
Pease Pottage Hill RH11: Craw 4F 21
PEASE POTTAGE SERVICE AREA 6F 21
Peeks Brook La. RH6: Ship B, Horl 3F 11
Peele Ho. RH13: Hors 5B 32
(off The Avenue)
Pegasus Ct. RH10: Craw 1B 20
RH14: Bill 2G 37
Pegasus Way RH19: E Grin 2H 25
Pegler Ct. RH10: Craw 5G 15
(off Pegler Way)
Pegler Way RH11: Craw 5G 15
Pegwell Cl. RH10: Craw 1C 20
Pelham Ct. RH11: Craw 3E 21
RH12: Hors 1F 33
Pelham Dr. RH10: Craw 3D 20
Pelham Pl. RH11: Craw 3E 21
Pembley Grn. RH10: Copt 6C 12
Pembroke Rd. RH10: Craw 2D 16
Penfold Rd. RH10: Craw 3C 22
Penn Cl. RH11: Craw 2G 15
Penn Ct. RH11: Craw 5C 14
Pennine Cl. RH11: Craw 5E 15
Penshurst Cl. RH10: Craw 4E 17
Peppard Rd. RH10: Craw 1E 23
Peppers Yd. RH12: Hors 6H 29
Percy Rd. RH12: Hors 6F 29
Perimeter Rd. RH6: Gatw 2C 10
Perimeter Rd. E. RH6: Gatw 4B 10
Perimeter Rd. Nth. RH6: Gatw 1G 9
Perimeter Rd. Sth. RH6: Gatw 4F 9
Perkstead Ct. RH11: Craw 2D 20
(off Kingsley Rd.)
Perry Av. RH19: E Grin 2E 25
Perryfield Ho. RH11: Craw 6G 15
(off Perryfield Rd.)
Perryfield Rd. RH11: Craw 6F 15
Perrylands RH6: Charlw 2C 8
Perrylands La. RH6: Horl 5C 6
Perth Cl. RH11: Craw 2G 15
Perth Way RH12: Hors 5B 30
Peterborough Rd. RH10: Craw 3H 21
Peterhouse Pde. RH10: Craw 2D 16
Peterlee Wlk. RH11: Craw 3B 20
Peters Cl. RH13: Southw 5C 36
Petworth Ct. RH11: Craw 2C 20
RH14: Bill 4H 37
(off Brooker's Rd.)
Petworth Dr. RH12: Hors 2B 30
Pevensey Cl. RH10: Craw 6D 16
Pevensey Rd. RH13: Southw 3B 36
Peverel Rd. RH11: Ifield 6B 14
Phillips Cl. RH10: Craw 4C 22
Phoenix La. RH19: Ash W 1E 27
Pickett's La. RH6: Gatw 3E 11
Picts Hill RH13: Hors 4E 33
Pigeon Pass RH10: Turn H 6H 19
Pine Cl. RH11: Craw 2F 15
RH14: Bill 2F 37
Pine Gdns. RH6: Horl 5F 5
Pine Gro. RH19: E Grin 2B 24
Pinehurst RH12: Hors 5G 29
Pines, The RH10: Worth 5E 17
RH12: Hors 4E 31
Pine Shaw RH10: Craw 4E 17
Pinetops RH12: Hors 4E 31
Pinetrees Cl. RH10: Copt 6A 12
Pine Way Cl. RH19: E Grin 6E 25
Pinewood Cl. RH12: Broadb H 6B 28
Pinova Cl. RH11: Ifield 2D 14
Pipers Cl. RH13: Southw 4B 36
Pippin Link RH11: Ifield 2D 14
Piries Pl. RH12: Hors 1G 33
(off Carfax)
PIXTON HILL .3H 27
Plantain Cres. RH11: Craw 3D 20
Plat, The RH12: Hors 6E 29
Platt Mdw. RH14: Bill 3F 37
Platts Rdbt. RH14: Bill 3F 37
Playden Ct. RH11: Craw 2C 20
Plough Cl. RH11: Ifield 3C 14
Plough La. RH12: Hors 4A 30
Plough Rd. RH6: Smallf 4E 7
Plover Cl. RH11: Craw 3F 15

Plovers Rd. RH13: Hors 6B 30
Poels Ct. RH19: E Grin 3E 25
Poles La. RH11: Low H 5F 9
Pollards RH11: Craw 6D 14
Pollards Dr. RH13: Hors 6A 30
Pond Cl. RH14: Bill 3F 37
Pond Farm Cl. RH13: Southw 2B 36
Pondtail Cl. RH12: Hors 3H 29
Pondtail Copse RH12: Hors 3H 29
Pondtail Dr. RH12: Hors 2H 29
Pondtail Pk. RH12: Hors 3H 29
Pondtail Rd. RH12: Hors 4G 29
Pond Way RH19: E Grin 4H 25
Pond Wood Rd. RH10: Craw 3B 16
Poplar Cl. RH11: Craw 2F 15
Poplar La. RH18: F Row 6E 27
Poplars, The RH13: Hors 6A 30
Poppy Cl. RH13: Southw 2C 36
Porchester Cl. RH13: Southw 3C 36
Portland Rd. RH19: E Grin 5E 25
Post Horn Cl. RH18: F Row 6H 27
Post Horn La. RH18: F Row 6G 27
Potter's Cft. RH13: Hors 1A 34
Pottersfield RH10: Craw 4G 15
Potters Pl. RH12: Hors 1G 33
POUND HILL .5D 16
Pound Hill Pde. RH10: Craw 4D 16
Pound Hill Pl. RH10: Craw 5D 16
Pound La. RH13: Mann H 5E 35
POVEY CROSS 6C 4
Povey Cross Rd. RH6: Horl 6C 4
Powell Cl. RH6: Horl 3D 4
Poynes Rd. RH6: Horl 2D 4
Poynings Rd. RH11: Ifield 6A 14
Premier Ho. RH10: Craw 1G 15
Premier Pde. RH6: Horl 4G 5
(off High St.)
Prestwick Cl. RH11: Ifield 6A 14
Prestwood Cl. RH11: Craw 2E 15
Prestwood La. RH11: Ifield 1A 14
Prewetts Mill RH12: Hors 2F 33
Priestcroft Cl. RH11: Craw 5D 14
Priestlands Cl. RH6: Horl 3E 5
Priestley Way RH10: Craw 1B 16
Primrose Av. RH6: Horl 6G 5
Primrose Cl. RH11: Craw 2E 21
Primrose Copse RH12: Hors 2H 29
Primrose La. RH18: F Row 6G 27
Princess Pct. RH6: Horl 4F 5
(off High St.)
Princess Rd. RH11: Craw 5F 15
Priors Wlk. RH10: Craw 5H 15
Priory Cl. RH6: Horl 3E 5
Priory Rd. RH18: F Row 6C 26
Proctor Cl. RH10: Craw 1D 22
Prospect Pl. RH11: Craw 5F 15
Pudding La. RH6: Charlw 1B 8
Puffin Hill RH10: Turn H 6H 19
Puffin Rd. RH11: Ifield 6A 14
Punch Copse Rd. RH10: Craw 4A 16
Punnetts Ct. RH11: Craw 2C 20
Purcell Rd. RH11: Craw 2C 20
Purley Cl. RH10: Craw 2E 23
Purton Rd. RH12: Hors 5F 29
Pyecombe Ct. RH11: Craw 2C 20

Q

Quadrangle, The RH6: Horl 4F 5
Quail Cl. RH12: Hors 2H 29
Quantock Cl. RH11: Craw 5E 15
Quarries, The RH13: Mann H 5F 35
Quarry Cl. RH11: Craw 3B 30
Quarry Ri. RH19: E Grin 2G 25
Quarry Way RH11: Craw 3B 36
Quarterbrass Farm Rd. RH12: Hors 2H 29
Quebec Cl. RH6: Smallf 4D 6
Queen's Ct. RH6: Horl 4F 5
Queen's Ga. RH6: Gatw 2B 10
Queens Pde. RH13: Hors 2H 33
(off Queen St.)
Queen's Rd. RH6: Horl 4F 5
RH19: E Grin 5E 25
Queen's Sq. RH10: Craw 5G 15
Queen St. RH13: Hors 2H 33
Queens Wlk. RH19: E Grin 4E 25

Queensway RH10: Craw 5H 15
RH13: Hors 2G 33
RH19: E Grin 4E 25
QUEEN VICTORIA HOSPITAL 2F 25
Questen M. RH10: Craw 3E 17

R

Racecourse Rd. RH6: Gatw 1A 10
Racecourse Way RH6: Gatw 1A 10
(off Nth. Terminal App.)
Rackham Cl. RH11: Craw 1G 21
Radford Rd. RH10: Craw 5C 10
Railey Rd. RH10: Craw 4H 15
Railway App. RH19: E Grin 4E 25
Rainbow Cl. RH6: Horl 2G 5
Rakers Ridge RH12: Hors 4H 29
Raleigh Ct. RH10: Craw 6B 10
Raleigh Dr. RH6: Smallf 4D 6
Raleigh Wlk. RH10: Craw 1H 21
Ramblers Way RH11: Craw 5E 21
Rampling Ct. RH10: Craw 6A 16
Ramsay Ct. RH11: Craw 4E 21
Ramsey Cl. RH6: Horl 4E 5
RH12: Hors 4H 29
Randall Scholfield Ct. RH10: Craw 4B 16
Ranmore Cl. RH11: Craw 5F 21
Ransome Ct. RH11: Craw 2B 20
Rascals Cl. RH13: Southw 6B 36
Rathbone Ho. RH11: Craw 4E 21
Rathlin Rd. RH11: Craw 2E 21
Raven Cl. RH10: Turn H 6H 19
RH12: Hors 3A 30
Ravendene Ct. RH11: Craw 6G 15
Raven La. RH11: Craw 3F 15
Ravenscroft Ct. RH12: Hors 6G 29
Rawlinson Rd. RH10: Craw 1E 23
Raworth Cl. RH10: Craw 1C 22
Raylands Pk. RH13: Southw 3D 36
Raymer Wlk. RH6: Horl 3H 5
Reapers Ct. RH12: Hors 4H 29
Rectory Flats RH11: Ifield 3C 14
Rectory La. RH6: Charlw 2A 8
RH11: Ifield 3C 14
Red Admiral St. RH12: Hors 3A 30
Red Deer Cl. RH13: Hors 6D 30
Redditch Cl. RH11: Craw 3B 20
Redehall Rd. RH6: Copt, Smallf 4E 7
Redford Av. RH12: Hors 5F 29
Redgarth Ct. RH19: E Grin 2B 24
Redgrave Dr. RH10: Craw 6E 17
Redkiln Cl. RH13: Hors 6B 30
Redkiln Cl. Ind. Est. RH13: Hors 5B 30
Redkiln Way RH13: Hors 5B 30
Red River Ct. RH12: Hors 4F 29
Redshank Ct. RH11: Ifield 6A 14
(off Stoneycroft Wlk.)
Redwing Cl. RH13: Hors 6B 30
Redwood Cl. RH10: Craw 3H 15
Reedings RH11: Ifield 1A 20
Reeds La. RH13: Southw 2D 36
Reeves Ho. RH10: Craw 5C 16
(off Trafalgar Gdns.)
Regal Dr. RH19: E Grin 5F 25
Regents Cl. RH11: Craw 3F 21
Regents M. RH6: Horl 4F 5
Reigate Cl. RH10: Craw 2E 17
Reigate Rd. RH2: Sid 1B 4
RH6: Hookw, Horl 3B 4
Renton Cl. RH14: Bill 3F 37
Reynard Cl. RH12: Hors 4D 30
Reynolds Pl. RH11: Craw 4F 15
Reynolds Rd. RH11: Craw 4F 15
Rhodes Way RH10: Craw 2A 22
Rices Hill RH19: E Grin 4F 25
Richardson Ct. RH11: Craw 4E 21
Richborough Ct. RH11: Craw 5F 15
Richmond Ct. RH10: Craw 6H 15
Richmond Rd. RH12: Hors 5G 29
Richmond Way RH19: E Grin 5F 25
Rickfield RH11: Craw 6D 14
RICKMANS GREEN 6E 11
Rickwood RH6: Horl 3G 5
Ridgehurst Dr. RH12: Hors 2D 32
Ridgeside RH10: Craw 5A 16
(not continuous)

Ridgeway RH19: E Grin 6E 25
Ridgeway, The RH6: Horl 6F 5
  RH12: Hors 5F 29
Ridgeway Ho. *RH6: Horl* *6F 5*
  (off The Crescent)
Ridings, The RH10: Craw 4E 17
Ridley Ct. RH10: Craw 2E 17
Ridleys Cnr. Rdbt. RH10: Craw 3E 17
Rillside RH10: Craw 2B 22
Rill Wlk. RH19: E Grin 4H 25
Rimmer Cl. RH11: Craw 5E 21
Ringley Av. RH6: Horl 4F 5
Ringley Oak RH12: Hors 5B 30
Ringley Rd. RH12: Hors 5A 30
Ring Rd. Nth. RH6: Gatw 1C 10
Ring Rd. Sth. RH6: Gatw 2D 10
Ringwood Cl. RH10: Craw 1H 21
Rise, The RH10: Craw 5D 16
  RH19: E Grin 5E 25
Ritchie Cl. RH10: Craw 3D 22
River Mead RH11: Ifield 2D 14
  RH12: Hors 2F 33
Riverside RH6: Horl 6F 5
  RH12: Hors 1E 33
  RH18: F Row 4E 27
Roberts Cl. RH13: Southw 1B 36
Robert Way RH12: Hors 2B 30
Robin Cl. RH11: Craw 3F 15
  RH13: Southw 3C 36
  RH19: E Grin 3F 25
Robin Hood La. RH12: Warnh 4C 28
Robin Hood Rdbt. RH12: Warnh 4F 29
Robin Row RH10: Turn H 6H 19
Robinson Ho. RH11: Craw 6G 15
Robinswood Ct. RH12: Hors 5B 30
Rockdene Cl. RH19: E Grin 4G 25
Rocks, The RH19: Ash W 1C 26
Roebuck Cl. RH13: Hors 5D 30
ROFFEY 5C 30
Roffey Cl. RH6: Horl 4E 5
ROFFEY PARK .3H 31
Roffey Pk. RH12: Colg 3G 31
Roffey's Cl. RH10: Copt 5H 11
Roffey Social and Sports Club *4C 30*
  (off Leith Vw. Rd.)
Roffye Ct. RH10: Craw 5C 30
Rokewood Dr. RH11: Ifield 2D 14
Roman Way RH14: Bill 2G 37
Rona Cl. RH11: Craw 2E 21
Rookery Hill RH1: Out 1D 6
  RH6: Out 1D 6
Rookery La. RH6: Out, Smallf 2D 6
Rook Way RH12: Hors 3B 30
Rookwood Golf Course 5E 29
Roosthole Hill RH13: Colg 3F 35
Ropeland Way RH12: Hors 2A 30
Rosamund Rd. RH10: Craw 1C 22
Rose Cotts. RH18: F Row 4E 27
Rosedale Cl. RH11: Craw 1D 20
Rosehill RH14: Bill 2G 37
Rosemary Ct. RH6: Horl 3D 4
Rosemary La. RH6: Charlw 2B 8
  RH6: Horl 5G 5
Rosemead Gdns. *RH10: Craw* *6H 15*
  (off Richmond Cl.)
Rose Wlk. RH11: Craw 1E 21
Rosier Commercial Cen.
  RH14: Bill 4H 37
Rosier Way RH14: Bill 5H 37
Roslan Ct. RH6: Horl 5G 5
Ross Cl. RH10: Craw 2A 22
Ross Ct. RH6: Horl 4G 5
Rossmore Cl. RH11: Craw 1E 17
Rother Cres. RH11: Craw 6C 14
Rothervale RH6: Horl 1F 5
Rough Fld. RH19: E Grin 1D 24
Rough Way RH12: Hors 4B 30
Roundabout Rd. RH10: Copt 5C 12
Roundstone Pk. RH13: Southw 2B 36
Roundway RH10: Craw 3G 15
Rowan Cl. RH10: Craw 5A 16
  RH12: Hors 4D 30
Rowan Ct. RH14: Bill 2G 37
Rowan Dr. RH14: Bill 2F 37
Rowan Wlk. RH10: Craw D 3H 19
Rowan Way RH12: Hors 4D 30

Rowena Ho. *RH11: Craw* *2G 15*
  (off Dobson Rd.)
ROWFANT 4C 18
Rowfant Bus. Cen. RH10: Rowf 5C 18
Rowfant Cl. RH10: Worth 5F 17
Rowland Cl. RH10: Copt 4D 12
Rowlands Rd. RH12: Hors 3C 30
Rowplatt Cl. RH19: Felb 6A 24
Rowplatt La. RH19: Felb 6A 24
Royal Ashdown Forest Golf Course 6G 27
Royal Oak Ho. RH10: Craw D 4G 19
Royce Rd. RH10: Craw 6B 10
Royston Cl. RH10: Craw 1B 16
Rudge Ho. *RH19: E Grin* *4F 25*
  (off Cantelupe Rd.)
Rudgwick Keep *RH6: Horl* *3H 5*
  (off Langshott La.)
Rudgwick Rd. RH11: Ifield 4C 14
Rufwood RH10: Craw D 3F 19
Runcorn Cl. RH11: Craw 3B 20
Runshooke Ct. RH11: Craw 2D 20
Runway Pk. RH11: Low H 4H 9
Rushams Rd. RH12: Hors 1F 33
Rushetts Pl. RH11: Craw 2F 15
Rushetts Rd. RH11: Craw 2E 15
Ruskin Cl. RH10: Craw 2D 16
Rusper Rd. RH11: Ifield 4A 14
  RH12: Hors 5B 30
Rusper Rd. Rdbt. RH12: Hors 2B 30
Ruspers Keep RH11: Ifield 4C 14
Russells Cres. RH6: Horl 5F 5
Russell Way RH10: Craw 6B 16
Russet Cl. RH6: Horl 4H 5
Russet Ct. RH13: Hors 5C 30
Russ Hill RH6: Charlw 4A 8
Russ Hill Rd. RH6: Charlw 3A 8
Ruston Ct. RH10: Craw 2D 22
Rutherford Way RH10: Craw 6B 10
Rutherford Way Ind. Est.
  RH10: Craw 6B 10
Rutherwick Cl. RH6: Horl 4E 5
Rutherwick Twr. RH6: Horl 4E 5
Rydal Cl. RH11: Ifield 1A 20
Ryders Way RH12: Hors 2B 30
Rye Ash RH10: Craw 4B 16
  (not continuous)
Ryecroft Dr. RH12: Hors 6E 29
Ryecroft Mdw. RH13: Mann H 5E 35
Ryelands RH6: Horl 3H 5
  RH11: Craw 6D 14
Ryst Wood Rd. RH18: F Row 5H 27

S

Sackville Cl. RH19: E Grin 2C 24
Sackville College 4F 25
Sackville Ct. RH19: E Grin 5F 25
Sackville Gdns. RH19: E Grin 2C 24
  (not continuous)
Sackville La. RH19: E Grin 2B 24
Saddler Row RH10: Craw 2G 21
Saddlers Cl. RH14: Bill 3F 37
St Agnes Ct. RH11: Craw 2D 20
St Aidan Cl. RH11: Craw 3E 25
St Andrews *RH6: Horl* *5G 5*
  (off Aurum Cl.)
St Andrews Rd. RH11: Ifield 6A 14
St Annes Rd. RH10: Craw 2D 16
St Aubin Ct. RH11: Craw 3C 20
St Augustine Rd. RH11: Craw 6E 15
St Barnabas Ct. RH10: Craw 4D 16
St Brelades Rd. RH11: Craw 3C 20
St Catherines Ct. RH19: E Grin 3D 24
ST CATHERINE'S HOSPICE (CRAWLEY)
  . . . . .1G 21
St Catherines Rd. RH10: Craw 2D 16
St Christopher's Cl. RH12: Hors 5G 29
St Clement Rd. RH11: Craw 3C 20
St Edmunds Cl. RH11: Craw 2G 15
St Edward's Cl. RH19: E Grin 4C 24
St Francis Gdns. RH10: Copt 5A 12
St Francis Wlk. RH11: Craw 1B 20
St Gabriels Rd. RH14: Bill 3G 37
St Georges RH6: Horl 5G 5
St Georges Cl. RH6: Horl 4G 5

St Georges Ct. RH10: Craw 4G 15
  RH19: E Grin 2C 24
St George's Gdns. RH13: Hors 5A 30
St Helier Cl. RH11: Craw 3D 20
St Hilda's Cl. RH6: Horl 4G 5
  RH10: Craw 2D 16
St Hughs Cl. RH10: Craw 2D 16
St Ives RH10: Craw 4D 16
St James Ct. RH19: E Grin 4D 24
St James Ho. RH19: E Grin 4E 25
St James Rd. RH19: E Grin 4E 25
St James Wlk. RH11: Craw 4F 21
St Joan Cl. RH11: Craw 2G 15
St John Cl. RH13: Hors 2A 34
St John's Cl. RH19: E Grin 3E 25
St John's Cres. RH12: Broadb H 6C 28
St John's Rd. RH11: Craw 5F 15
  RH19: E Grin 3E 25
St Leonard's Dr. RH11: Craw 1B 22
ST LEONARDS FOREST 5G 31
ST LEONARD'S PARK 1D 34
St Leonards Pk. RH19: E Grin 4E 25
St Leonard's Rd. RH13: Hors 3A 34
St Margaret's Rd.
  RH19: E Grin 2F 25
St Mark's La. RH12: Hors 3A 30
St Mary's Cl. RH14: Bill 3G 37
St Mary's Dr. RH10: Craw 3C 16
St Mary's Gdns. RH12: Hors 2G 33
St Mary's Ho. *RH12: Hors* *2G 33*
  (off Normandy)
St Mary's Wlk. RH12: Hors 2G 33
St Michaels Rd. RH19: E Grin 3E 25
St Nicholas Ct. RH10: Craw 4D 16
St Peter's Rd. RH11: Craw 5F 15
St Richard's M. *RH10: Craw* *5A 16*
  (off Broomdashers Rd.)
St Sampson Rd. RH11: Craw 3C 20
St Swithun's Cl. RH19: E Grin 4F 25
St Vincent Cl. RH10: Craw 6E 17
St Wilfrid's Way RH11: Craw 6E 15
Salehurst Rd. RH10: Worth 5F 17
Salisbury Ct. *RH13: Southw* *3C 36*
  (off Porchester Cl.)
Salisbury Rd. RH10: Craw 3H 21
  (not continuous)
  RH13: Hors 3E 33
Saltdean Cl. RH10: Craw 2G 21
Salterns Rd. RH10: Craw 2D 22
Salvington Rd. RH11: Craw 2C 20
Samaritan Cl. RH11: Craw 1B 20
Samphire Cl. RH11: Craw 2D 20
Sandeman Way RH13: Hors 3A 34
Sandhawes Hill RH19: E Grin 1G 25
Sandhill La. RH10: Craw D 4G 19
Sandown Ct. RH10: Craw 5E 17
Sandpiper Cl. RH11: Ifield 1A 20
Sandringham Cl. RH19: E Grin 5G 25
Sandringham Rd. RH11: Craw 3E 21
Sandy Cl. RH10: Craw D 3F 19
Sandy La. RH10: Craw D 3F 19
  RH19: E Grin 4E 25
San Feliu Ct. RH19: E Grin 3H 25
Sangers Dr. RH6: Horl 4E 5
Sangers Wlk. RH6: Horl 4E 5
Sarel Way RH6: Horl 2G 5
Sargent Cl. RH10: Craw 3A 22
Sark Cl. RH11: Craw 3D 20
Satellite Bus. Village
  RH10: Craw 1H 15
Saturn Cl. RH11: Craw 1B 20
Saunders Cl. RH10: Craw 5C 16
Savernake Wlk. RH10: Craw 2A 22
Saville Gdns. RH14: Bill 4G 37
Saxley RH6: Horl 3H 5
Saxon Cl. RH14: Bill 2G 37
  (not continuous)
Saxon Cres. RH12: Hors 5F 2
Saxon Rd. RH10: Worth 6F 1
Sayers, The RH19: E Grin 4C 2
Sayers Cl. RH13: Hors 1A 3
Scallows Cl. RH10: Craw 4B 1
Scallows Rd. RH10: Craw 4B 1
Schaffer Cl. RH10: Craw 1D 2
Schlumberger Ho. RH6: Gatw 2D 1
School Cl. RH12: Hors 3C 3
School Hill RH12: Warnh 1D 2

School La.—Stonebridge Ct.

School La. RH14: Bill 2H **37**
RH18: F Row 5F **27**
RH19: Ash W 1D **26**
School Wlk. RH6: Horl 4D **4**
Scory Cl. RH11: Craw 2D **20**
Scott Rd. RH10: Craw 2A **22**
Scott's Hill RH1: Out 1G **7**
Seaford Rd. RH11: Craw 4D **20**
Searle's Vw. RH12: Hors 4A **30**
Seddon Ct. RH11: Craw 4E **21**
Sedgefield Cl. RH10: Craw 4F **17**
Sedgewick Cl. RH10: Craw 5D **16**
Sedgwick La. RH13: Hors 6B **34**
Selbourne Cl. RH10: Craw 1E **17**
Selham Cl. RH11: Craw 4D **14**
Selsey Ct. RH11: Craw 3E **21**
Selsey Rd. RH11: Craw 3D **20**
Selwyn Cl. RH10: Craw 2D **16**
Sequoia Pk. RH11: Craw 1G **21**
Serrin Way RH12: Hors 4A **30**
Severn Rd. RH10: Craw 6D **16**
Sewill Cl. RH6: Charlw 2C **8**
Seymour Rd. RH11: Craw 3D **20**
Shackleton Rd. RH10: Craw 2H **21**
Shaftesbury Rd. RH10: Craw 1E **23**
Shalesbrook La. RH18: F Row 6F **27**
Shandys Cl. RH12: Hors 2E **33**
Sharon Cl. RH10: Craw 2B **22**
Sharpthorne Cl. RH11: Ifield 5C **14**
Shaw's La. RH13: Southw 4A **36**
Shaws Rd. RH10: Craw 4A **16**
Shearwater Ct. *RH11: Ifield* *6A 14*
(off Stoneycroft Wlk.)
Sheffield Cl. RH10: Craw 1C **22**
Sheldon Cl. RH10: Craw 6E **17**
Shelley Cl. RH10: Craw 3D **16**
Shelley Dr. RH12: Broadb H 6A **28**
Shelley Rd. RH12: Hors 6F **29**
RH19: E Grin 4C **24**
Shelleys Ct. RH13: Hors 5C **30**
Shepherd Cl. RH10: Craw 2H **21**
Shepherds Way RH12: Hors 4C **30**
Sheppey Cl. RH11: Craw 2E **21**
Sheraton Wlk. RH11: Craw 4E **21**
Sheridan Pl. RH19: E Grin 4C **24**
Shermanbury Ct. *RH12: Hors* *5H 29*
(off Blenheim Rd.)
Sherwood Wlk. RH10: Craw 2A **22**
Shetland Cl. RH10: Craw 4F **17**
Shinwell Wlk. RH11: Craw 4E **21**
SHIPLEY BRIDGE **3G 11**
Shipley Bri. La. RH6: Ship B 4G **11**
RH10: Ship B 4G **11**
Shipley Rd. RH11: Craw 4D **14**
RH13: Southw 6B **36**
Ship St. RH19: E Grin 5E **25**
Shire Pde. RH10: Craw 4E **17**
Shire Pl. *RH10: Craw* *4E 17*
(off Byerley Way)
Shirley Cl. RH11: Craw 3A **20**
Shoreham Rd. RH10: Craw 2D **22**
Short Cl. RH11: Craw 2G **15**
Short Gallop RH10: Craw 4E **17**
Shortsfield Cl. RH12: Hors 4G **29**
Shottermill RH12: Hors 2C **30**
Shovelstrode La. RH19: Ash W, E Grin . . .5H **25**
Sideways La. RH6: Hookw 6B **4**
Siena Dr. RH10: Craw 1E **17**
Silchester Dr. RH11: Craw 2E **21**
Silkin Wlk. RH11: Craw 4D **20**
Silver Birch Ho. RH11: Craw 4F **21**
Silver Ct. RH19: E Grin 3C **24**
Silver La. RH14: Bill 4G **37**
Silverlea Gdns. RH6: Horl 5H **5**
Silverwood Ind. Est.
RH10: Craw D 6E **13**
Sinclair Cl. RH10: Craw 1D **22**
Singleton Rd. RH12: Broadb H 6A **28**
Siskin Av. RH10: Turn H 6H **19**
Siskin Cl. RH12: Hors 4A **30**
Sissinghurst Cl. RH10: Craw 4E **17**
Skelmersdale Wlk. RH11: Craw 3B **20**
Skipton Way RH6: Horl 2G **5**
Skylarks RH14: Bill 4F **37**
Skylark Vw. RH12: Hors 2H **29**
Slaugham Ct. RH11: Craw 2C **20**
Sleets Rd. RH12: Broadb H 6C **28**
Slinfold Wlk. RH11: Craw 5D **14**
(not continuous)
Sloughbrook Cl. RH12: Hors 3B **30**
SMALLFIELD **4E 7**
Smallfield Rd. RH6: Horl 4G **5**
(not continuous)
RH6: Horne, Smallf 4G **7**
Smallmead RH6: Horl 4G **5**
Small's La. RH11: Craw 5F **15**
Smalls Mead RH11: Craw 5F **15**
Smeeds Cl. RH19: E Grin 2G **25**
Smithbarn RH13: Hors 6C **30**
Smithbarn Cl. RH6: Horl 3G **5**
Smith Cl. RH10: Craw 2G **21**
Smolletts RH19: E Grin 5C **24**
Snell Hatch RH11: Craw 5E **15**
Snowdrop Cl. RH11: Craw 3D **20**
SNOW HILL **5F 13**
Snow Hill RH10: Craw D 6E **13**
Snowhill Bus. Cen. RH10: Copt 5F **13**
Snowhill La. RH10: Copt, Craw D 4E **13**
Soane Cl. RH11: Craw 1B **20**
Somergate RH12: Hors 1D **32**
Somerville Dr. RH10: Craw 2D **16**
Sorrel Cl. RH11: Craw 3D **20**
Sorrell Rd. RH12: Hors 4A **30**
Southbrook RH11: Craw 4F **21**
South Cl. RH10: Craw 4A **16**
Southdown Cl. RH12: Hors 4C **30**
SOUTHGATE **1H 21**
Southgate Av. RH10: Craw 6H **15**
Southgate Dr. RH10: Craw 1G **21**
Southgate Pde. RH10: Craw 1G **21**
Southgate Rd. RH10: Craw 1G **21**
Southgate Rdbt. RH11: Craw 2F **21**
South Gro. RH13: Hors 2H **33**
Sth. Holmes Rd. RH13: Hors 5D **30**
Southlands RH6: Horl 4E **5**
RH19: E Grin 6E **25**
Southlands Av. RH6: Horl 3E **5**
South Pde. RH6: Horl 3E **5**
Sth. Perimeter Track RH6: Gatw 4E **9**
Sth. Pier Rd. RH6: Gatw 2C **10**
South St. RH12: Hors 2G **33**
Southview Cl. RH10: Copt 6D **12**
Southwark Cl. RH11: Craw 3E **21**
SOUTHWATER **3C 36**
Southwater Bus. Pk. RH13: Southw 4B **36**
Southwater Cl. RH11: Craw 5D **14**
Southwater Country Pk. **5B 36**
Southwater Leisure Cen. **4B 36**
SOUTHWATER STREET **2C 36**
Southwater St. RH13: Southw 2B **36**
Southways Pk. RH10: Low H 6G **9**
Southwell Cotts. RH6: Charlw 2B **8**
Southwick Cl. RH19: E Grin 3D **24**
Spartan Way RH11: Ifield 2D **14**
Speedwell Way RH12: Hors 4A **30**
Spencers Pl. RH12: Hors 5F **29**
Spencers Rd. RH11: Craw 6F **15**
RH12: Hors .6F **29**
Spiers Farm Cl. RH6: Horl 5G **5**
Spiers Way RH6: Horl 6G **5**
Spindle Way RH10: Craw 6A **16**
Spinney, The RH6: Horl 2F **5**
RH11: Craw .1E **21**
Spinney Cl. RH10: Craw D 3H **19**
RH12: Hors .3D **30**
Spooners Indoor Bowls Club **6E 25**
Spooners Rd. RH12: Hors 5C **30**
Spring Cl. RH11: Craw 6G **15**
Spring Copse RH10: Copt 6B **12**
RH19: E Grin 2F **25**
Springfield RH19: E Grin 1D **24**
Springfield Ct. RH11: Craw 6G **15**
RH12: Hors .1G **33**
Springfield Cres. RH12: Hors 1F **33**
Springfield Gdns. RH19: Felb 6B **24**
Springfield La. RH12: Colg 6H **31**
Springfield Pk. RH12: Hors 6G **29**
Springfield Pk. Rd. RH12: Hors 1F **33**
Springfield Rd. RH11: Craw 6F **15**
RH12: Hors .1F **33**
(not continuous)
Spring Gdns. RH10: Copt 6B **12**
RH12: Hors .6G **29**
Spring Mdw. RH18: F Row 6F **27**
Spring Plat RH10: Craw 5D **16**
Spring Plat Ct. RH10: Craw 5D **16**
Spring Wlk. RH6: Horl 4E **5**
Spring Way RH19: E Grin 1G **25**
Spruce Pl. RH19: E Grin 2G **25**
Spurgeon Cl. RH11: Craw 4F **15**
Square, The RH10: Craw 5G **15**
Squires, The RH11: Pease P 6E **21**
Squires Cl. RH10: Craw D 3F **19**
Squirrel Cl. RH11: Craw 2E **15**
Squirrel Ridge RH10: Craw D 4G **19**
Stable Cl. RH10: Craw 2E **23**
Stable Cotts. RH11: Pease P 5D **20**
Stable Flats RH11: Pease P 5D **20**
Stace Way RH10: Craw 3F **17**
Stackfield Rd. RH11: Ifield 6B **14**
Stafford Rd. RH11: Craw 2D **14**
Staffords Pl. RH6: Horl 6G **5**
Stagelands RH11: Craw 3E **15**
Stagelands Ct. RH11: Craw 3F **15**
Stakers La. RH13: Southw 4C **36**
Stanbridge Cl. RH11: Ifield 5B **14**
Standen Cl. RH19: E Grin 2A **24**
Standen Pl. RH12: Hors 2C **30**
Standinghall La. RH10: Turn H 2H **23**
Stane St. RH14: Adv, Bill 6E **37**
RH14: Bill 1H **37**
Stanford Ct. *RH10: Craw* *1D 22*
(off Maidenbower Pl.)
Stanford Orchard RH12: Warnh 1D **28**
Stanford Way RH12: Broadb H 6B **28**
Stan Hill RH6: Charlw 1A **8**
Stanier Cl. RH10: Craw 6C **16**
Stanley Cen. RH10: Craw 2A **16**
Stanley Cl. RH10: Craw 1H **21**
Stanley Wlk. RH13: Hors 1H **33**
Stan's Way RH12: Hors 1G **33**
Staplecross Ct. RH11: Craw 2D **20**
Star Cl. RH13: Hors 5C **30**
Station App. RH6: Horl 4G **5**
Station App. Rd. RH6: Gatw 1C **10**
Station Cl. RH13: Hors 1H **33**
Station Cotts. RH13: Hors 4B **32**
Station Hill RH10: Craw 4C **16**
Station Rd. RH6: Horl 4G **5**
RH10: Craw .6G **15**
RH10: Craw D 3G **19**
RH12: Warnh 1E **29**
RH13: Hors .5B **32**
(Christ's Hospital Rd.)
RH13: Hors .1H **33**
(Station Cl.)
RH13: Southw 4B **36**
RH14: Bill 3G **37**
RH18: F Row 4F **27**
RH19: E Grin 4D **24**
Station Rd. Sth. RH13: Southw 4B **36**
Station Way RH10: Craw 6G **15**
Steers La. RH10: Craw 5D **10**
Stemp Dr. RH14: Bill 3F **37**
Stennings, The RH19: E Grin 3C **24**
Stephen Cl. RH11: Craw 2G **15**
Stephenson Dr. RH19: E Grin 6F **25**
Stephenson Pl. RH10: Craw 5C **16**
Stephenson Way RH10: Craw 5B **16**
Stephenson Way Ind. Est. RH10: Craw . . .5C **16**
Stepney Cl. RH10: Craw 1D **22**
Sterling Bldgs. *RH12: Hors* *1G 33*
(off Carfax)
Sterling Pk. RH10: Craw 6C **10**
Stevenage Rd. RH11: Craw 2B **20**
Steyning Cl. RH10: Craw 3H **15**
Stildon M. RH19: E Grin 2C **24**
Stirling Cl. RH10: Craw 6C **16**
Stirling Pl. RH12: Broadb H 6B **28**
Stirling Way RH13: Hors 1A **34**
RH19: E Grin 2H **25**
Stirrup Way RH10: Craw 4E **17**
Stoat Ho. RH11: Craw 2E **15**
Stockfield RH6: Horl 3G **5**
Stocks Cl. RH6: Horl 5G **5**
Stockwell Cen. RH10: Craw 5B **16**
Stockwell Rd. RH19: E Grin 6E **25**
Stokers Cl. RH6: Gatw 1H **9**
Stokes Cl. RH10: Craw 1D **22**
Stonebridge Ct. RH11: Craw 3F **21**
RH12: Hors .1E **33**

Stone Ct. RH10: Worth 5E 17
Stonecourt Cl. RH6: Horl 4H 5
Stonecrop Cl. RH11: Craw 2E 21
Stonedene Cl. RH18: F Row 5H 27
Stonefield Cl. RH10: Craw 6G 15
Stoneleigh Cl. RH19: E Grin 4F 25
Stonepark Dr. RH18: F Row 5G 27
STONEQUARRY 1G 25
Stoneybrook RH12: Hors 2D 32
Stoneycroft Wlk. RH11: Ifield 6A 14
Stopham Rd. RH10: Craw 2D 22
Storrington Ct. RH11: Craw 4D 14
Strachey Cl. RH11: Craw 4E 21
Strand Cl. RH10: Craw 1E 23
Strathmore Rd. RH11: Ifield 2D 14
Strawson Ct. RH6: Horl 3E 5
Stream Pk. RH19: E Grin 2A 24
Street, The RH6: Charlw 2B 8
Street Hill RH10: Worth 6F 17
Strickland Cl. RH11: Ifield 6B 14
STROOD GREEN 3A 28
Strood La. RH12: Broadb H, Warnh . . .2A 28
Stroudley Cl. RH10: Craw 6C 16
Stroudley Ct. RH19: E Grin 3F 25
(off Badger's Way)
Strudgate Cl. RH10: Craw 1C 22
Stuart Cl. RH10: Craw 6D 16
Stuart Way RH19: E Grin 6F 25
Stubfield RH12: Hors 6E 29
Stubpond La. RH7: Newchap 1H 13
Stumblets RH10: Craw 4D 16
Suffolk Cl. RH6: Horl 5F 5
Sullington Hill RH11: Craw 1G 21
Sullington Mead RH12: Broadb H 6C 28
Sullivan Dr. RH11: Craw 2B 20
Summer Ho. RH11: Craw 6F 15
(off Oak Rd.)
Summersvere Cl. RH10: Craw 2B 16
Sundew Cl. RH11: Craw 3D 20
Sunningdale Ct. RH10: Craw 1G 21
Sunny Av. RH10: Craw D 3F 19
Sunnyhill Cl. RH10: Craw D 3F 19
Sunnymead RH10: Craw D 3G 19
(not continuous)
RH11: Craw 5G 15
SUNNYSIDE 6E 25
Sunoak Rd. RH13: Hors 1E 35
Surrenden Ri. RH11: Craw 5F 21
Surrey & Sussex Crematorium
RH10: Craw 1E 17
Sussex Ct. RH13: Hors 2H 33
RH14: Bill 4H 37
(off Brooker's Rd.)
Sussex Lodge RH12: Hors 5G 29
Sussex Manor Bus. Pk.
RH10: Craw 1B 16
Sutton M. RH19: E Grin 4F 25
Suva Rd. RH19: E Grin 2C 24
Swaledale Cl. RH11: Craw 2F 21
Swallowfield Cl. RH13: Mann H 6E 35
Swallow Fld. Copse RH13: Southw . . .2C 36
Swallowfields RH6: Horl 4G 5
(off Rosemary La.)
Swallow Rd. RH11: Craw 3F 15
Swallow St. RH10: Turn H 6H 19
Swallowtail Rd. RH12: Hors 3A 30
Swan Cl. RH13: Southw 3C 36
Swan La. RH6: Charlw 2C 8
Swann Way RH12: Broadb H 6C 28
Swans Ghyll RH18: F Row 4E 27
Swan Sq. RH12: Hors 1G 33
Swan Wlk. RH12: Hors 1G 33
Swift La. RH11: Craw 3F 15
Swindon Rd. RH12: Hors 5F 29
Sycamore Av. RH12: Hors 3E 31
Sycamore Cl. RH11: Craw 2F 15
Sycamore Dr. RH19: E Grin 4G 25
Sylvan Rd. RH10: Craw 1B 22
Symonds Ho. RH11: Ifield 2D 14

T

Talbot La. RH12: Hors 2G 33
Tallis Cl. RH11: Craw 2C 20
Tall Trees RH19: E Grin 5F 25
Talman Cl. RH11: Ifield 6B 14

Tamar Cl. RH10: Craw 6D 16
Tanbridge Ho. RH12: Hors 2F 33
Tanbridge Pk. RH12: Hors 2E 33
Tanbridge Pl. RH12: Hors 2F 33
Tanbridge Retail Pk. RH12: Hors 2F 33
Tangle Oak RH19: Felb 6A 24
Tangmere Rd. RH11: Craw 5C 14
Tanyard Ct. RH13: Hors 2H 33
Tanyard Av. RH19: E Grin 5G 25
Tanyard Ct. RH10: Craw 2D 22
RH13: Hors 2A 34
Tanyard Way RH6: Horl 2G 5
Target Hill Local Nature Reserve 3C 20
Tarham Cl. RH6: Horl 2D 4
Tatham Ct. RH11: Craw 4E 21
Taunton Cl. RH10: Craw 4E 17
Taylor Wlk. RH11: Craw 5F 15
Teal Cl. RH12: Hors 4G 29
Teasel Cl. RH11: Craw 2E 21
Teesdale RH11: Craw 2F 21
Telford Pl. RH10: Craw 6H 15
Telham Ct. RH11: Craw 2C 20
Temple Cl. RH10: Craw 6E 17
Tennyson Cl. RH10: Craw 3C 16
RH12: Hors 3A 30
Tennyson Ri. RH19: E Grin 4C 24
Tern Rd. RH11: Ifield 6A 14
Terry Rd. RH11: Craw 4E 21
Testers Cl. RH13: Southw 6B 36
Thatcher Cl. RH10: Craw 2G 21
Thatchers Cl. RH6: Horl 2G 5
RH12: Hors 5A 30
The . . . .
Names prefixed with 'The' for example
'The Acorns' are indexed under the main
name such as 'Acorns, The'
Thelton Av. RH12: Broadb H 6B 28
Thetford Wlk. RH11: Craw 3B 20
Theydon Cl. RH10: Craw 1B 22
Thirlmere Rd. RH11: Ifield 1A 20
Thistle Way RH6: Smallf 4F 7
RH13: Southw 2C 36
Thomson Ct. RH11: Craw 4E 21
Thorndyke Cl. RH10: Craw 6E 17
Thornhill RH11: Craw 1E 21
Thornton Cl. RH6: Horl 4D 4
Thornton Ho. RH13: Hors 5B 32
(off The Avenue)
Thornton Pl. RH6: Horl 4D 4
Thornton Wlk. RH6: Horl 4D 4
Three Acres RH12: Hors 2E 33
THREE BRIDGES 4B 16
Three Bridges Rd. RH10: Craw 5A 16
Three Bridges Station (Rail) 5C 16
Threestile Rd. RH12: Warnh 1D 28
Ticehurst Cl. RH10: Worth 5F 17
TILGATE 2H 21
Tilgate Dr. RH10: Craw 6B 16
(Hylands Cl.)
RH10: Craw 3G 21
(The Avenue, not continuous)
Tilgate Forest (Forest Gate) Business Cen.
RH11: Craw 4G 21
Tilgate Forest Golf Course 3B 22
Tilgate Forest Theatre 4H 21
Tilgate Mans. RH10: Craw 4A 22
Tilgate Nature Pk. 4H 21
Tilgate Pde. RH10: Craw 2H 21
Tilgate Park (Country Park) 4H 21
Tilgate Pl. RH10: Craw 2H 21
Tilgate Way RH10: Craw 2H 21
Tilletts La. RH12: Warnh 1C 28
Tillotson Cl. RH10: Craw 6E 17
Tiltwood Dr. RH10: Craw D 2H 19
Timber Cl. RH10: Craw 6G 29
Timberham Farm Rd. RH6: Gatw 1G 9
Timberham Way RH6: Gatw 1H 9
Timberlands RH11: Craw 4E 21
Timber Mill RH13: Southw 3B 36
Timbers, The RH13: Mann H 5E 35
RH19: E Grin 3C 24
Tinsley Cl. RH10: Craw 2B 16
TINSLEY GREEN 5C 10
Tinsley Grn. RH10: Craw 5C 10
Tinsley La. RH10: Craw 1B 16
Tinsley La. Nth. RH10: Craw 6C 10

Tinsley La. Sth. RH10: Craw 3B 16
(off Hazelwick Av.)
Tintagel Ct. RH13: Hors 2H 33
Tintern Rd. RH11: Craw 1D 20
Tiree Path RH11: Craw 2E 21
Tithe, The RH11: Craw 2D 14
Tithe Orchard RH19: Felb 6A 24
Titmus Dr. RH10: Craw 2A 22
Todds Cl. RH6: Horl 2D 4
Toftwood Cl. RH10: Craw 6D 16
Tollgate Hill RH11: Craw 5F 21
Tollgate Hill Rdbt. RH11: Craw 5E 21
Tollgate Pl. RH19: E Grin 5F 25
(off Lewes Rd.)
Tomlin Ct. RH10: Craw 5A 16
TOMPSET'S BANK 6F 27
Tompset's Bank RH18: F Row 6F 27
Tomtit Cres. RH10: Turn H 6H 19
Tom Tits La. RH18: F Row 6E 27
Toronto Dr. RH6: Smallf 4D 6
Tourist Info. Cen.
Crawley 6H 15
Horsham 2G 33
Tower App. Rd. RH6: Gatw 3H 9
Tower Cl. RH6: Horl 4E 5
RH13: Hors 3E 33
RH19: E Grin 3E 25
Tower Ct. RH13: Hors 2G 33
RH19: E Grin 3E 25
(off Tower Cl.)
TOWER HILL 3E 33
Tower Hill RH13: Hors 5D 32
Tower Rd. RH12: Fay, Colg 1H 31
Town Barn Rd. RH11: Craw 5F 15
Townland RH14: Bill 2G 37
Town Mead RH11: Craw 4G 15
Townsend Way RH10: Craw 1E 23
Trafalgar Gdns. RH10: Craw 4C 16
Trafalgar Rd. RH12: Hors 5G 29
Treadcroft Dr. RH12: Hors 4A 30
Treetops RH13: Southw 4H 35
Treeview RH11: Craw 4F 21
Trefoil Cl. RH12: Hors 4A 30
Trefoil Cres. RH11: Craw 3D 20
Trenear Cl. RH13: Hors 1A 34
Trent Cl. RH11: Craw 1C 20
Trevanne Plat RH10: Craw 4E 17
Trewaren Ct. RH11: Craw 5F 15
Treyford Cl. RH11: Craw 5C 14
Trinity Cl. RH10: Craw 3D 16
Trinity Ct. RH10: Craw 6G 29
Trinity Sq. RH13: Hors 1H 33
Trist Way RH11: Craw 3D 14
Troon Cl. RH11: Ifield 6A 14
Trotton Cl. RH10: Craw 2D 22
Trundle Mead RH12: Hors 4G 29
Tudor Cl. RH6: Smallf 4E 7
RH10: Craw 6E 17
RH19: E Grin 5F 25
Tuggles Plat RH12: Warnh 2C 28
Tulip Ct. RH12: Hors 5G 29
Tullett Rd. RH10: Craw 3C 22
Tunnel Rd. RH6: Gatw 1H 9
Tunnmeade RH11: Ifield 6B 14
Turner Av. RH14: Bill 4F 37
Turner Ct. RH19: E Grin 5F 25
Turners Cl. RH13: Southw 5C 36
TURNERS HILL 6E 19
Turners Hill Pk. RH10: Turn H 6H 19
Turners Hill Rd. RH10: Craw D, Turn H .6D 12
RH10: Craw, Worth 5E 17
RH19: E Grin 6C 24
Turner Wlk. RH10: Craw 2A 22
Turnpike Pl. RH11: Craw 3G 15
Turret Ct. RH19: E Grin 2C 24
Turtledove Av. RH10: Turn H 6H 19
Tuscany Gdns. RH10: Craw 2H 15
Tushmore Av. RH10: Craw 2H 15
Tushmore Ct. RH10: Craw 3H 15
Tushmore Cres. RH10: Craw 2G 15
Tushmore La. RH10: Craw 3H 15
Tushmore Rdbt. RH10: Craw 3G 15
Tussock Cl. RH11: Craw 1D 21
Tuxford Cl. RH10: Craw 1D 21
Tweed La. RH11: Ifield 2C 14
Twitten, The RH11: Craw 5F 15
Twitten La. RH19: Felb 6A 24

Two Mile Ash Rd.—Windmill Cl.

Two Mile Ash Rd. RH13: Hors, Southw . . . 2A **36**
Twyhurst Ct. RH19: E Grin . . . 2D **24**
Twyne Cl. RH11: Craw . . . 1C **20**
Twyner Cl. RH6: Horl . . . 3A **6**
Tylden Way RH12: Hors . . . 3B **30**
Tyler Rd. RH10: Craw . . . 2G **21**
Tymperley Ct. *RH13: Hors . . . 6A **30***
(off Kings Rd.)
Tyne Cl. RH10: Craw . . . 6D **16**

U

Underwood Cl. RH10: Craw D . . . 3G **19**
Upfield RH6: Horl . . . 5F **5**
Upfield Cl. RH6: Horl . . . 6F **5**
Uppark Gdns. RH12: Hors . . . 3B **30**
Upper Cl. RH18: F Row . . . 5F **27**
Upper Sq. RH18: F Row . . . 4F **27**

V

Vale Dr. RH12: Hors . . . 1F **33**
Vallance By-Ways Gatwick RH6: Charlw . . . 3C **8**
Vanbrugh Cl. RH11: Craw . . . 2B **20**
Vancouver Ct. RH6: Smallf . . . 4D **6**
Vancouver Dr. RH11: Craw . . . 2G **15**
Vanners RH10: Craw . . . 4H **15**
Vector Point RH10: Craw . . . 1A **16**
Verbania Way RH19: E Grin . . . 4H **25**
Vernon Cl. RH12: Hors . . . 5C **30**
Vicarage La. RH6: Horl . . . 3E **5**
Vicarage Rd. RH10: Craw D . . . 4F **19**
Vicarage Wlk. RH19: E Grin . . . 4F **25**
Victor Ct. RH10: Craw . . . 2E **17**
Victoria Cl. RH6: Horl . . . 4F **5**
Victoria Ct. RH13: Hors . . . 1H **33**
Victoria M. RH11: Craw . . . 5G **15**
Victoria Rd. RH6: Horl . . . 4F **5**
RH11: Craw . . . 5F **15**
Victoria Sq. *RH6: Horl . . . 4F **5***
(off Consort Way)
Victoria St. RH13: Hors . . . 1H **33**
Victoria Ter. RH19: E Grin . . . 2E **25**
Victoria Way RH19: E Grin . . . 6F **25**
Victory Rd. RH12: Hors . . . 6F **29**
Viking Ho. RH6: Low H . . . 4G **9**
Vinall Gdns. RH12: Broadb H . . . 5B **28**
Vincent Cl. RH13: Hors . . . 1B **34**
Virgin Active
Crawley . . . **4G 15**
Vivienne Cl. RH11: Craw . . . 2G **15**
Vulcan Cl. RH11: Craw . . . 3F **21**

W

Waddington Cl. RH11: Craw . . . 2D **20**
Wadeys, The RH14: Bill . . . 3F **37**
Wadham Cl. RH10: Craw . . . 2D **16**
Wagg Cl. RH19: E Grin . . . 4G **25**
Wagtail Cl. RH12: Hors . . . 2H **29**
Wain End RH12: Hors . . . 4H **29**
Wainwrights RH10: Craw . . . 2G **21**
Wakefield Ct. RH12: Hors . . . 1F **33**
Wakehams Grn. Dr. RH10: Craw . . . 2E **17**
Wakehurst Dr. RH10: Craw . . . 2G **21**
Wakehurst M. RH12: Hors . . . 2D **32**
Waldby Ct. RH11: Craw . . . 2D **20**
Walesbeech RH10: Craw . . . 6B **16**
Walhatch Cl. RH18: F Row . . . 5F **27**
Walker Rd. RH10: Craw . . . 1C **22**
Wallage La. RH10: Craw D, Rowf . . . 5B **18**
WALL HILL . . . **3E 27**
Wall Hill Rd. RH19: Ash W, F Row . . . 2D **26**
Wallis Ct. RH10: Craw . . . 1A **16**
Wallis Ho. *RH19: E Grin . . . 4E **25***
(off Orchard Way)
Wallis Way RH13: Hors . . . 5C **30**
Walmer Cl. RH13: Southw . . . 3C **36**
Walnut Ct. RH13: Hors . . . 2A **34**
Walnut La. RH11: Craw . . . 2E **15**
Walnuts, The RH12: Hors . . . 5G **29**
Walstead Ct. RH10: Craw . . . 6G **15**
Walstead Ho. RH10: Craw . . . 6G **15**
Walton Dr. RH13: Hors . . . 5D **30**
Walton Heath RH10: Craw . . . 3E **17**
Wandle Cl. RH10: Craw . . . 6D **16**
Wantage Cl. RH10: Craw . . . 2D **22**
Warbleton Ho. *RH11: Craw . . . 2C **20***
(off Breezehurst Dr.)
Warburton Cl. RH19: E Grin . . . 4G **25**
Wareland Ho. *RH19: E Grin . . . 4E **25***
(off Railway App.)
Warltersville Way RH6: Horl . . . 6H **5**
Warner Cl. RH10: Craw . . . 3D **22**
WARNHAM . . . **1D 28**
Warnham Ct. RH12: Warnh . . . 2D **28**
Warnham Ct. M. RH12: Warnh . . . 2D **28**
Warnham Mnr. RH12: Warnh . . . 2A **28**
Warnham Nature Reserve . . . **4F 29**
Warnham Park . . . **3D 28**
Warnham Rd. RH10: Craw . . . 1B **22**
RH12: Broadb H . . . 5B **28**
RH12: Warnh, Hors . . . 4F **29**
Warnham Station (Rail) . . . **1G 29**
Warren Cl. RH19: Felb . . . 6A **24**
Warren Dr. RH11: Craw . . . 4D **14**
RH13: Southw . . . 2B **36**
Warrington Cl. RH11: Craw . . . 3B **20**
Washington Rd. RH11: Craw . . . 2B **20**
Wassand Cl. RH10: Craw . . . 5B **16**
Watercress Pl. RH13: Hors . . . 6B **30**
Waterfield Cl. RH13: Hors . . . 6A **30**
Waterfield Gdns. RH11: Craw . . . 1B **20**
Water Lea RH10: Craw . . . 6B **16**
Waterside RH6: Horl . . . 2F **5**
RH19: E Grin . . . 4H **25**
Waterside Cl. RH11: Craw . . . 1B **20**
Water Vw. RH6: Horl . . . 4A **6**
Waterworks Cl. RH18: F Row . . . 3F **27**
Watson Cl. RH10: Craw . . . 1D **22**
Waveney Wlk. RH10: Craw . . . 1C **22**
Waverley Ct. RH12: Hors . . . 1F **33**
Wavertree Ct. *RH6: Horl . . . 5E **5***
(off Massetts Rd.)
Wayside RH11: Ifield . . . 1B **20**
Weald, The RH19: E Grin . . . 1F **25**
Weald Cl. RH13: Hors . . . 3A **34**
Weald Ct. Rd. RH14: Bill . . . 4G **37**
Weald Dr. RH10: Craw . . . 6B **16**
Wealden Ho. RH19: E Grin . . . 1C **26**
Wealdon Cl. RH13: Southw . . . 5B **36**
WEATHERHILL . . . **4D 6**
Weatherhill Cl. RH6: Horl . . . 4C **6**
Weatherhill Rd. RH6: Horl, Smallf . . . 4C **6**
Weaver Cl. RH11: Ifield . . . 6B **14**
Webb Cl. RH11: Craw . . . 4E **21**
Weddell Rd. RH10: Craw . . . 2A **22**
Weirbrook RH10: Craw . . . 2B **22**
WEIR WOOD . . . **5B 26**
Weir Wood Reservoir . . . **4A 26**
Weir Wood Sailing Club . . . **4B 26**
Weller Cl. RH10: Worth . . . 6E **17**
Wellfield RH19: E Grin . . . 6H **25**
Wellingham Way RH12: Fay . . . 3A **20**
Wellington Cl. RH10: Craw . . . 2F **17**
Wellington Ga. RH19: E Grin . . . 2G **25**
Wellington Rd. RH12: Hors . . . 1H **33**
Wellington Town Rd.
RH19: E Grin . . . 3D **24**
Wellington Way RH6: Horl . . . 2E **5**
Wells Cl. RH12: Hors . . . 1D **32**
Wells Lea RH19: E Grin . . . 2D **24**
Wells Mdw. RH19: E Grin . . . 2D **24**
Wells Rd. RH10: Craw . . . 3H **21**
Wellwood Cl. RH13: Hors . . . 5D **30**
Welwyn Cl. RH11: Craw . . . 3B **20**
Wenlock Cl. RH11: Craw . . . 1D **20**
Wensleydale RH11: Craw . . . 2F **21**
Wentworth Dr. RH10: Craw . . . 4E **17**
Wesley Cl. RH6: Horl . . . 2F **5**
RH11: Craw . . . 2B **20**
West Av. RH10: Craw . . . 3B **16**
Westbrook RH18: F Row . . . 4E **27**
Westcott Cl. RH11: Craw . . . 5F **21**
Westcott Keep *RH6: Horl . . . 3H **5***
(off Langshott La.)
Westfield Rd. RH11: Craw . . . 5E **15**
WEST GREEN . . . **4F 15**
West Green Dr. RH11: Craw . . . 4F **15**
West Green Pk. . . . **4F 15**
West Gun Copse RH13: Hors . . . 6B **32**
West Hill RH19: E Grin . . . 5D **24**
Westlands RH13: Hors . . . 6A **30**
West La. RH19: E Grin . . . 5D **24**
Westleas RH6: Horl . . . 2D **4**
West Leigh RH19: E Grin . . . 6E **25**
West Meads RH6: Horl . . . 4H **5**
Westminster Rd. RH10: Craw . . . 6D **16**
Westons Cl. RH12: Hors . . . 2H **29**
West Pde. RH12: Hors . . . 5G **29**
West Pk. Rd. RH7: Newchap . . . 4E **13**
RH10: Copt, Newchap . . . 5E **13**
West St. RH11: Craw . . . 6G **15**
RH12: Hors . . . 1G **33**
RH14: Bill . . . 3F **37**
RH19: E Grin . . . 5E **25**
West Vw. Gdns. RH19: E Grin . . . 5E **25**
West Way RH10: Craw . . . 4B **16**
Westway RH6: Gatw . . . 2C **10**
RH10: Copt . . . 6G **11**
Wheatfield Way RH6: Horl . . . 2G **5**
Wheatsheaf Cl. RH12: Hors . . . 4A **30**
Wheatstone Cl. RH10: Craw . . . 6C **10**
Wheeler Rd. RH10: Craw . . . 1C **22**
Wheelers La. RH6: Smallf . . . 5D **6**
Wheelers Way RH19: Felb . . . 6A **24**
Whistler Cl. RH10: Craw . . . 2A **22**
Whitecroft RH6: Horl . . . 3G **5**
Whitehall Dr. RH11: Ifield . . . 5B **14**
Whitehall Pde. *RH19: E Grin . . . 4E **25***
(off London Rd.)
White Hart Ct. RH12: Hors . . . 5G **29**
Whitehorse Rd. RH12: Hors . . . 3D **30**
White House, The RH10: Craw . . . 6G **9**
WHITELY HILL . . . **4G 23**
Whitely Hill RH10: Worth . . . 4G **23**
Whitewalls *RH11: Craw . . . 5C **14***
(off Rusper Rd.)
Whitgift Wlk. RH10: Craw . . . 2G **21**
Whitmore Way RH6: Horl . . . 3D **4**
Whittington College RH19: Felb . . . 1A **24**
Whittington Rd. RH10: Craw . . . 2G **21**
Whittle Way RH10: Craw . . . 5B **10**
Whitworth Rd. RH11: Craw . . . 1G **15**
Whytings RH13: Mann H . . . 5E **35**
Wickham Cl. RH6: Horl . . . 3E **5**
Wickhurst Gdns. RH12: Broadb H . . . 6C **28**
Wickhurst La. RH12: Broadb H . . . 6C **28**
Wickland Ct. RH10: Craw . . . 2G **21**
Wicks Rd. RH14: Bill . . . 3F **37**
Widgeon Way RH12: Hors . . . 4G **29**
Wilberforce Cl. RH11: Craw . . . 5F **21**
Wilberforce Way RH13: Southw . . . 1C **36**
Wilderwick Rd. RH19: E Grin . . . 1G **25**
Wildgoose Dr. RH12: Hors . . . 6D **28**
Wild Orchid Way RH13: Southw . . . 2C **36**
Wild Wood RH12: Hors . . . 6D **28**
Wilkinson Ct. RH11: Craw . . . 4E **21**
Willard Way RH19: E Grin . . . 2A **24**
William Gdns. RH6: Smallf . . . 4D **6**
William Morris Way
RH11: Craw . . . 5E **21**
Williams Way RH10: Craw . . . 5C **16**
Willow Brean RH6: Horl . . . 3D **4**
Willow Cl. RH10: Craw . . . 3H **15**
RH19: E Grin . . . 2D **24**
Willow Cnr. RH6: Charlw . . . 2C **8**
Willow Ct. RH6: Horl . . . 1G **5**
Willow Dr. RH14: Bill . . . 3G **37**
Willowfield RH11: Craw . . . 6F **15**
Willow Mead RH19: E Grin . . . 5F **25**
Willow Rd. RH12: Hors . . . 4D **30**
Willows, The RH12: Hors . . . 4H **29**
RH14: Bill . . . 4F **37**
Wilmington Cl. RH11: Craw . . . 4E **21**
Wilmot's La. RH6: Horne . . . 1G **7**
Wilson Cl. RH10: Craw . . . 2E **23**
Wilton Ho. RH11: Craw . . . 5F **15**
Wimblehurst Ct. RH12: Hors . . . 5G **29**
Wimblehurst Rd. RH12: Hors . . . 5G **29**
Wimbourne Ho. RH11: Craw . . . 5F **15**
Wimland Rd. RH12: Fay . . . 2E **31**
Wincanton Cl. RH10: Craw . . . 4E **17**
Winchester Ct. *RH13: Southw . . . 3C **36***
(off Porchester Cl.)
Winchester Rd. RH10: Craw . . . 3H **21**
Windmill Cl. RH6: Horl . . . 4G **5**
RH13: Hors . . . 5C **30**

A-Z Crawley 55

Windmill Ct. RH10: Craw 3G 15
Windmill La. RH19: E Grin 2D 24
(Goodwins Cl.)
RH19: E Grin 1C 26
(Wellfield)
Windrum Cl. RH12: Hors 3D 32
Windrush Cl. RH11: Craw 1C 20
Windsor Cl. RH11: Craw 3F 21
RH13: Southw 4C 36
Windsor Ct. RH13: Hors 6B 30
Windsor Pl. RH10: Craw 1A 16
RH19: E Grin 5G 25
Windyridge RH11: Craw 6D 14
Winfield Way RH11: Craw 3F 21
Winner Way RH6: Gatw 3G 9
Winnet Way RH13: Southw 3C 36
Winterbourne RH12: Hors 2B 30
Winterfold RH10: Craw 2B 22
Winter Gdns. RH11: Craw 6F 15
Winterpit Cl. RH13: Mann H 5F 35
Winterpit La.
RH13: Mann H, Plum P 5F 35
Winterton Ct. RH13: Hors 1H 33
Wisborough Ct. RH11: Craw 2C 20
Wiston Ct. RH11: Craw 2C 20
RH12: Hors ....
(off Woodstock Cl.)
Wither Dale RH6: Horl 3D 4
Withey Brook RH6: Hookw 6C 4
Withey Mdws. RH6: Hookw 6C 4
Woburn Rd. RH11: Craw 1D 20
Wold Cl. RH11: Craw 1C 20
Woldhurstlea Cl. RH11: Craw 1D 20
Wolstonbury Cl. RH11: Craw 1F 21
Wolverton Cl. RH6: Horl 6E 5
Wolverton Gdns. RH6: Horl 5E 5
Woodbridge Ct. RH12: Hors 4C 30
Woodbury Av. RH19: E Grin 3H 25
Woodbury Cl. RH19: E Grin 5G 25
Woodcote RH6: Horl 3G 5
Woodcote Rd. RH18: F Row 5E 27
Woodcourt RH11: Craw 4F 21
Woodcroft Rd. RH11: Ifield 1A 20
Wood End RH12: Hors 4E 31
Woodend Cl. RH10: Craw 3B 16

Woodfield RH13: Southw 4B 36
Woodfield Cl. RH10: Craw 4H 15
Woodfield Lodge RH10: Craw 3B 16
Woodfield Rd. RH10: Craw 4H 15
Woodgates Cl. RH13: Hors 6B 30
Woodhatch RH13: Southw 3B 36
Woodhayes RH6: Horl 3G 5
Wooding Gro. RH11: Craw 4E 21
Woodland Cl. RH13: Hors 5D 30
Woodland Dr. RH10: Craw D 3G 19
Woodlands RH6: Horl 3H 5
RH10: Craw 3E 17
Woodlands, The RH6: Smallf 4E 7
Woodlands Cl. RH10: Craw D 4G 19
Woodlands Rd. RH19: E Grin 1G 25
Woodlands Wlk. RH13: Mann H 6E 35
Woodlands Way RH13: Southw 5A 36
RH14: Bill 5H 37
Woodland Way RH13: Hors 5C 30
Woodmancote Ct. RH12: Hors 4H 29
(off Blenheim Rd.)
Woodmans Hill RH11: Craw 4F 21
Woodpeckers RH13: Southw 2B 36
Woodpecker Way RH10: Turn H 6H 19
Woodroffe Benton Ho.
RH11: Craw 5C 14
(off Rusper Rd.)
Woodroyd Av. RH6: Horl 5E 5
Woodroyd Gdns. RH6: Horl 6E 5
Woods Hill Cl. RH19: Ash W 1D 26
Woods Hill La. RH19: Ash W 1D 26
Woodside RH13: Hors 5D 30
Woodside Cres. RH6: Smallf 4D 6
Woodside Rd. RH10: Craw 3A 16
Woodstock RH19: E Grin 3C 24
Woodstock Cl. RH12: Hors 4H 29
Wood St. RH19: E Grin 4D 24
Woodwards RH11: Craw 4E 21
Woolborough Cl. RH10: Craw 4H 15
Woolborough La. RH10: Craw 2A 16
Woolborough Rd. RH10: Craw 4G 15
Worcester Rd. RH10: Craw 3H 21
Wordsworth Cl. RH10: Craw 3C 16
Wordsworth Pl. RH12: Hors 2A 30
Wordsworth Ri. RH19: E Grin 4C 24

Worsted La. RH19: E Grin 5H 25
WORTH 5F 17
WORTH ABBEY 4H 23
Worth Ct. RH10: Turn H 4H 23
Worthing Rd. RH12: Hors 5E 33
RH13: Hors 5E 33
RH13: Southw ....2B 36 & 6C 36
Worth Pk. Av. RH10: Craw 4C 16
Worth Rd. RH10: Craw 4D 16
Worth Way
RH10: Craw D, Rowf 4E 19
RH10: E Grin 4A 24
RH10: Rowf, Worth 5A 18
RH10: Worth 6F 17
Wray Cl. RH19: Ash W 1D 26
WRAYS 3A 4
Wren Cl. RH12: Hors 2H 29
Wren Ct. RH10: Craw 2H 21
Wren St. RH10: Turn H 6H 19
Wright Cl. RH10: Craw 3C 22
Wroxham Wlk. RH10: Craw 1C 22
Wycliffe Ct. RH11: Craw 2B 20
Wye Cl. RH11: Craw 5F 21
Wynlea Cl. RH10: Craw D 3F 19
Wysemead RH6: Horl 3H 5
Wyvern Pl. RH12: Warnh 1D 28

Y

Yarmouth Cl. RH10: Craw 1B 22
Yarrow Cl. RH12: Hors 4A 30
Yattendon Rd. RH6: Horl 4G 5
Yew Ct. RH11: Craw 6G 15
(off Springfield Rd.)
RH19: E Grin 3C 24
Yewlands Wlk. RH11: Ifield 1A 20
Yew La. RH19: E Grin 2B 24
Yew Tree Cl. RH6: Horl 2E 5
Yew Tree Ct. RH6: Horl 3F 5
Yew Tree Rd. RH6: Charlw 2B 8
York Av. RH19: E Grin 5F 25
York Cl. RH13: Hors 6B 30
RH13: Southw 4C 36
York Rd. RH10: Craw 3H 21

SAFETY CAMERA INFORMATION

PocketGPSWorld.com's CamerAlert is a self-contained speed and red light camera warning system for SatNavs and Android or Apple iOS smartphones/tablets. Visit www.cameralert.co.uk to download.

Safety camera locations are publicised by the Safer Roads Partnership which operates them in order to encourage drivers to comply with speed limits at these sites. It is the driver's absolute responsibility to be aware of and to adhere to speed limits at all times.

By showing this safety camera information it is the intention of Geographers' A-Z Map Company Ltd., to encourage safe driving and greater awareness of speed limits and vehicle speed. Data accurate at time of printing.

Printed and bound in the United Kingdom by Gemini Press Ltd., Shoreham-by-Sea, West Sussex
Printed on materials from a sustainable source